God, Science, and the Supernatural

God, Science, and the Supernatural

Randy Fisk

God, Science, and the Supernatural

Copyright © 2019 by Randy Fisk
Second Printing 2022

Published by Second Ref Press, Mapleton, Illinois 61547
SecondRefPress.com

ISBN: 978-0-578-53253-0

All Scripture quotations, unless otherwise indicated, are taken from the HOLY BIBLE, NEW INTERNATIONAL VERSION®. NIV®. Copyright © 1973, 1978, 1984, 2011 by Biblica, Inc®. Used by permission of Zondervan. All rights reserved.

Scripture references marked KJV are from the King James Version of the Bible. Those marked NKJV are from the New King James Version®. Copyright © 1984 by Thomas Nelson, Inc. Used by permission. All rights reserved.

All rights reserved. This book may not be reproduced in any form for commercial gain or profit. Copying short quotations or occasional pages is permitted and encouraged. Otherwise seek the permission of the author.

For inquiries about the book or availability to teach, the author may be contacted at *RandyFisk333@gmail.com*.

Cover design by Keith Lang. The infrared photograph of the Orion Nebula is from the Cambridge Astronomical Survey Unit, ESO/J. Emerson/VISTA.

Edited by Holly Brooks.

Printed in the United States of America

*Dedicated to
My Daughters and Sons-in-Law:*

Mandy and Justice—
Revivalists and Seekers of Wisdom

Becky and Keith—
Worshippers and Bringers of His Presence

Holly and Ken—
Filled with Creativity, Prophetic Insight, and Healing

Acknowledgments

I would like to thank my wonderful wife Mary for her encouragement, perceptiveness, and the journey we walk together, all of which were a great help in writing this book. I would also like to thank my three daughters and their husbands for their insights and for being the amazing people they are. I also appreciate my many friends, colleagues, and pastors—notably Mike Smith and John King: remarkable pastors with hearts of gold, who pushed me forward to know more and more of God. And I would like to express my gratitude to the people of both the Vineyard Church of Aurora, Illinois and Riverside Community Church in Peoria, Illinois for their encouragement and the good time we had together as I developed and refined this material. Special thanks to Holly Brooks for the exceptional way she edited this book, the many hours she spent on it, and the joy it was to work together with her! Also, many thanks to Keith Lang for the beautiful book cover he created. Thanks, too, to Justice Perhay for all the conversations we had about the subjects covered in this book. Finally, I would like to thank my Lord and God, who always gives me more than I ask. God, You are truly amazing.

Contents

Foreword 11
Introduction 13

1   Curiosity 19

Part I: Time

2   God and Time 31
3   Walking in the Now and Not Yet 47

Part II: Space

4   God and Space 59
5   Walking in God's Presence 69

Part III: Matter

6   God and What Fills the Universe 85
7   Partnering with His Voice 97

Part IV: Energy

8   God, Energy and Motion 111

Part V: The Realm Outside the Natural

9   Science vs. Christianity 125
10 Seeing the Supernatural 137
11 What is Most Important to God 147

Bibliography 158
About the Author 161

Foreword

When Randy handed me the manuscript of *God, Science, and the Supernatural* to review, I felt honoured but totally unqualified to do so! But this is the amazing fact of this book: whether you feel qualified or not, it will draw you in.

It is written in such a way that even the person feeling unqualified to read a book about science and the supernatural is suddenly pulled into reading it. This is because the book is written by a writer who not only knows about science in a deep way but also experiences the supernatural in such amazing ways! He lives for the presence of God because He has experienced it in very real ways. Link this into his scientific mind and suddenly you are seeing the Super becoming very Natural!

The reality becomes obvious that science is linked with the supernatural because our creator God made the science of creation and also brings His presence into that creation. This is just great thinking and reading.

Randy Fisk came into my life a few years ago. I immediately knew we would click and become friends. His humble loving personality, linked with a deep love of Jesus and a desire to see people helped, healed and blessed, just shone out of this man, in my mind making him a wonderful man of God.

It is a privilege to write this foreword to a great book that takes the reader further than maybe they have been before... right into God's very presence, and once you're there, anything can happen! Enjoy the adventure!

John King
Lead Pastor, Riverside Community Church
Peoria, IL

Introduction

A fish, aside from when it jumps out of the water, would have a difficult time imagining what any realm besides water is like. So it is with us who are confined to the realm of time and three-dimensional space. It is difficult to comprehend what time and space really are, let alone conceive of a reality outside of them. However, Scripture describes the realm of God as being outside of time as we know it and not confined to the world that we experience.

In the past 120 years, science has found that space and time are not what they appear to be. Also, the substance of what fills this universe, at the most fundamental level, is vastly different than what we previously imagined. Although this book talks a lot about recent science, please understand that I am not using it to interpret Scripture. Rather, I am using it to open our minds—to make us realize that time and space are different from what we may have thought—and then take our open minds to Bible verses that touch upon the realm of God. I am trying to approach Scripture with no preconceived notions about anything; I am just seeing what it says on its own. Just as Biblical scholars remind us that we should set aside our worldviews and cultural biases to fully grasp the meanings of words first spoken to cultures different from our own, so we must set aside our confined views of reality to appreciate some rather staggering concepts that Scripture presents about God.

This book is written to students of both science and theology. To the former, one of the premises of this book is that without God, and without an appreciation of the realm in which He operates, we severely limit the reality there is to explore. Said another way, those who feel that science, and the physical realm in which it functions, is the only truth worthy of seeking, need to know that there is a fascinating reality that they are missing. To students of theology who take a nineteenth-century understanding of the universe to their interpretation of the Bible, without seeing the mind-boggling concepts it contains about space and time, I say that your view of God is simply too small. To both groups, a world of discovery awaits that is fascinating, eye-opening, and something that can lead us to a world beyond our dreams.

Throughout my years as a Christian, I often have discovered things in Scripture that were there all along, but that I simply did not have the worldview to see. Discovering such things has made my life in the Lord a fascinating journey. I am still learning things that are thoroughly Scriptural, but that require a new perspective in order to better incorporate them into my life. That is part of the adventure God calls us to live, and one that often bears much fruit.

It is this heart—which seeks and examines notions that may be new to us yet are clearly Scriptural—that I want us to have, as we break down the boundaries of our understanding of just who God is and the way He wants us to see reality. My hope is that this will not only bring an appreciation of the new things we may discover along the way, but that it also will build our faith and make us more effective in expanding His kingdom.

My Own Journey

My background is in high energy physics. This type of physics involves accelerating protons so close to the speed of light that, instead of making them go faster (they cannot exceed the speed of light), the energy added to them goes into increasing their mass, often by a factor of many thousands. This requires particle accelerators like those at CERN in Switzerland and Fermilab in Illinois, the latter being the facility where I worked. As protons smash into each other at such high energies, sometimes new particles are formed for a brief period of time, their existence determined from looking at their decay products. Thus, our understanding of the fundamental building blocks of the universe can grow.

During my years in school, I had a thirst to know truth. I could see that the beauty and unanswered questions that physics uncovered pointed to something (or *Someone*) beyond the realm of physics. But I did not know what (or *Who*) that was. I had written off Christianity—from my limited experience as a youngster, I viewed it more as a social club and felt that they didn't even do *that* very well! This point of view was about to change, however.

When I met Mary, who is now my wife, and her impassioned pastor, Theodore Laesch, my misconception of Christianity was totally transformed. What I now heard about God was too beautiful and too different to be attributed to man. During the time I was considering all these things, a Presence was invading my world, bringing me to a confrontation not just with intellectual ideas, but also with a world (or kingdom) that I knew I had to enter. And I knew that entering it would change everything. That change, I would find out, was for the better—much better than I had ever thought possible. I would never want to go back to the ways things were before, which were far inferior. So, to all those inferior ways, which I could see included sinful and selfish attitudes that would have led me to a sad and shallow life, I said "good riddance." I also found that to make this possible, it cost the King whom I had encountered an enormous price. But welcoming this King, receiving what He had paid so dearly for, and embracing His kingship, breathed life into me in a way I had never thought possible. Everything was new.

This all happened when I was a graduate student in high energy physics, soon to get my doctorate and pursue post-doctoral research. In trying to explain what Christianity was about, my understanding was somewhat underdeveloped, but I was passionate about the new life I was enjoying every day. Strangely wonderful things happened. I was approached by a writer from the *Slavic Gospel Association* who asked me to record my story so they could broadcast it behind the Iron Curtain. This was to counter Soviet propaganda saying that Christianity was at odds with science, and that no scientist believed it. A collection of these recordings, made by various scientists, eventually was formed into a book called *Scientists Who Believe*. I was honored to be in such a book and found myself among names such as James Irwin (the Apollo 15 astronaut) and C. Everett Koop (the U.S. Surgeon General at that time). In my story I had said that Albert Einstein felt that there must be a Creator, although not one (he thought) that he could know personally. Since I had found a personal relationship with God, the editor added that I had "gone beyond Einstein" in this, which eventually was set as the title of my chapter. This has always bothered me, striking me as being a bit like a musician writing a book called "Beyond Beethoven." No respectable musician would do that! It was true, however, that you *can* know the Creator of the universe personally, and I had done that.

As my life progressed, I went to seminary, became a professor of physics at Valparaiso University, and later became associate pastor at the Vineyard Christian Fellowship in Elgin, Illinois. Eventually I felt that I was most useful in helping other pastors equip their people by teaching them to better hear from the Lord and effectively partner with Him in healing. So that is what I have continued to do.

Every so often I talked about my scientific background and, when I did, received such a positive response (even from those who had little exposure to science in school), that I realized it was filling a vacuum that was out there. Many people have been led to believe that science leaves no room to believe in a divine being. When I countered this, and even used science to show not only that God is real, but also that everything about Him is awesome, it resonated with all who heard it. (The first time I broached this subject, I jokingly asked the ushers to lock the

Introduction 17

doors so that no one could escape! I was happy to find out that no one wanted to leave, and even wanted to hear more!)

   Speaking on what became some of the chapters of this book, even I was surprised at how well the topics that I covered were evidenced in so many verses, giving different perspectives of the natural and supernatural realms. Much like a physics book, this book is broken into parts such as *Time*, *Space*, and *Matter*. Most of these parts contain two chapters. The first chapter in each part examines some of the latest developments in physics (all of which are well accepted in the scientific community but may be new to some of the readers) and compares them with ideas and verses that Scripture presents. Where, at one time, some thought that science and Christianity were add odds with one another, we are finding out that, more and more, science is in agreement with what Scripture has said all along. The alternate chapters within each part then look at the ministry of Jesus, and the ministry He has given to us, focusing especially on their supernatural aspects. Even though, at first glance, it may seem that the discussions about science and the supernatural are an odd combination, I do this for several reasons. In light of people misusing science to belittle Christianity, with the supernatural aspect of it taking the greatest beating, I find it useful to not only defend the supernatural aspects of Christianity, but to go even further to show how they dovetail with the fascinating things that both science and Scripture have to say. This encourages us to remove the limitations we sometimes place on the ministry that Jesus modeled, as we respond to His invitation to take part in it ourselves. I'm hoping that what I say in this book will increase our understanding, faith, and partnership with God in ministry. For in partnering with Him, we get to touch His realm, which is beyond the reality we know—a realm that is both different and wonderful.

1
Curiosity

Before I get into time, space, and what fills the universe, I'd like to take a look at the subject of curiosity. One of the current attacks against Christianity is the attempt to characterize Christians as being against curiosity and science. This, as will be discussed below, is far from the truth. It stands opposed to the fact that many of the great scientists throughout history were vibrant Christians, their Christianity propelling them in their quest to learn more. We will see that God likes us to be curious, and it is one of the ways He gets us to dig into the treasure trove of things He wants to reveal to us. He looks forward to seeing the delight of discovery on our faces. That is the delight I am aiming to see as we explore the topics of this book.

Curiosity and Science

Neil deGrasse Tyson is one of the most well-known scientists and frequently quoted spokespersons for the scientific community. Perhaps what he is most passionate about is curiosity. He delights in admitting what he does not know, using it to illustrate how curiosity fuels the pursuit of scientific exploration. Indeed, when I was a professor of physics, if I could stoke students' curiosity, then they would be more likely to learn on their own and absorb things much more efficiently. For me, instilling curiosity was a goal even greater than imparting knowledge, for that would cause them to grow in many different fields of endeavor and improve many aspects of their lives.

Tyson has commented about negative reactions he has received from some Christians who feel that "God did it" is a sufficient answer to the questions of the universe. Although I don't know Tyson's feelings about this well, I suspect that the divide between him and Christians is exaggerated by others more than himself, those others having the agenda of showing that science is anti-God or that Christianity is anti-science. To those who hold this point of view, I would say several things: First, not all Christians use God as an excuse not to be curious. Those who feel this way are a minority. There are also many non-Christians who refuse to be curious. Second, Christianity actually promotes curiosity. Scripture shows that God loves our seeking Him and being fascinated by all He has created (more on that later). Third, in our scientific pursuits, if we try to keep God out of the picture, we are limiting ourselves, closing ourselves off from an amazing, fascinating realm. There is way more to discover here! Curiosity should include pondering more than just the physical realm.

So, in this chapter, I want to show how curiosity (and words that are related to it) are so emphasized by God.

Curiosity in Scripture

The concept of curiosity is discussed in Scripture using several different words, each representing different stages of discovery. **Curiosity** often has to do with something so unknown that we might not know quite what we are looking for. It pushes us to ask questions and explore the unknown. The word **seeking** comes into play once we have discovered something…now we are after it; we want to know more. **Desiring** represents a passion to find what we are seeking. We are willing to pay a price to find it. Finally, **hunger** represents a desire at an even deeper level; there is an inner drive, even desperation, for something. Scripture has instances of each of these, showing how highly God values curiosity, even going beyond simple curiosity in intensity.

Curiosity

The concept of **curiosity** was expanded for me in an interview I once saw with Donald Rumsfeld, the former U.S. Secretary of Defense. He said there are two categories of what we don't know: (1) what we *know* we don't know, and (2) what we *don't know* we don't know. (He called these *known unknowns* and *unknown unknowns*.) For example, he said that he knew there were probably terrorist cells in the United States but didn't know where. This is the first category of what we do not know; they are *known unknowns*, and there are ways to look for them. What really worried him, however, is that there might be other threats that were so unknown that the Defense Department would not even know what to look for. This is the second category of the unknown: *unknown unknowns*. These are too far off the radar; they are so unknown that we have no grid for them. Scripture has examples of these. Consider this:

"Call to me and I will answer you and tell you great and unsearchable things you do not know." (Jeremiah 33:3)

Here God is saying there are things we do not know—unsearchable things (unknown unknowns), so off our radar that we don't know we don't know them. He wants us to seek Him for these things. But how? We don't even know what question to ask, so the only thing to do is to call on Him to show them to us!

An example of encountering something unexpected is this:

There the angel of the Lord appeared to him in flames of fire from within a bush. Moses saw that though the bush was on fire it did not burn up. So Moses thought, "I will go over and see this strange sight—why the bush does not burn up." When the Lord saw that he had gone over to look, God called to him from within the bush, "Moses! Moses!" And Moses said, "Here I am." (Exodus 3:2-4)

Here is an example of God using curiosity to draw someone to Himself. It shows that He must value curiosity, since He uses it to cause people to get to know Him. In my own life, this is one of the ways He drew me to Himself. I knew there had to be something more and was fascinated and curious what that "something more" might be. C.S. Lewis, in *The Lion, the Witch and the Wardrobe*—an allegory about discovering God and His kingdom—shows this concept well, as the children's journey began with their insatiable curiosity as to what was in the world on the other side of the wardrobe.

The very fact that God is *awesome* means that we become full of awe at seeing something mind-boggling. This is the emotion that comes on the tail of curiosity, as the discovery of what we see produces wonder and surprise. I once heard someone describe how he pictured the angels in heaven crying, "Holy!" as they beheld the Lord. The word "holy" means "set apart"—something so different that it is in a category of its own. It produces awe. It struck him that, essentially, they were saying, "Whoa!"—an exclamation of being overwhelmed by a sight of such uniqueness that it would prompt amazement, although they had seen it countless times before and would react the same way countless times afterward.

The concept of **seeking** is about our pressing into something once we have begun to discover it. The most well-known examples of this are these words of Jesus:

> *"But seek first his kingdom and his righteousness, and all these things will be given to you as well." (Matthew 6:33)*

> *"Ask and it will be given to you; seek and you will find; knock and the door will be opened to you." (Matthew 7:7)*

Here Jesus is encouraging us to be curious and press in. The kingdom is worthy of our seeking it with all we are worth.

Even more intensive is this:

> ***He is a rewarder of those who diligently seek Him.*** *(Hebrews 11:6, NKJV)*

Here we are encouraged to seek God *diligently*. And God says there will be a reward in doing so. (This is also a great way to approach reading God's Word! There will be rewards when we do—something He is going to show us.)

Beyond seeking is ***desiring***. As Paul says, this can apply to desiring both God and the things of God:

> ***Follow the way of love and eagerly desire gifts** [literally: the things] **of the Spirit, especially prophecy.*** *(1 Corinthians 14:1)*

Here the Greek word for *eagerly desire* is so intense, it is translated "covet" in other places. While it is wrong to covet the things of this world that are not ours, it is fine (and commanded) to eagerly desire God and the things of His Spirit.

Beyond desiring is ***hunger or thirst***, as is illustrated by these words of David:

> ***As the deer pants for streams of water, so my soul pants for you, my God. My soul thirsts for God, for the living God. When can I go and meet with God?*** *(Psalm 42:1-2)*

In many ways, hunger is the most precious commodity a person can have, since it leads that person to more. Paradoxically, finding more of God can leave us deeply satisfied yet even hungrier for more. It is interesting that God leads us to Himself through curiosity, seeking, desire, and hunger. Our coming to God is not like getting a theology book with all the questions answered. Rather, it is an introduction to the most intriguing, fascinating, captivating, good, and awesome Person we could ever know; and that introduction sets us on a journey to pursue Him, which will change our lives forever.

First and Second-Generation Prophets

The topics of seeking, desiring, and hungering for more of God are illustrated in Scripture by the examples of first-generation prophets. First-generation prophets, in the way I am defining them, are those such as Moses, Elijah, Samuel, and Isaiah, who became such by seeking God for themselves. Second-generation prophets ride on the coattails of first-generation prophets, their pools of knowledge coming from what the first generation said and experienced. Generally, they are not as willing to risk failure as first-generation prophets. They tend not to deviate from the ways and customs of their teachers, even if they don't understand where those ways and customs came from. [Note: In looking at the ways and customs we may encounter, some may be good, some neutral, and some hindrances, but we must go back to the source to find out where they came from and whether they are the best choices to follow in our present circumstances. For example, a revivalist of the past may have spoken in a loud, agitated voice, but we may find that does not fit our personality or is not effective in reaching the people we are called to reach.] Of course, it is good to learn from others and honor those who have gone before us, but not at the expense of not seeking things out for ourselves. As we seek God ourselves, we may arrive at our own ways of doing things. But the important thing is that our heart and passion will be driven by God, whom we have sought and encountered personally—the heart and passion of a first-generation prophet. Such a passion will be difficult to extinguish.

Elisha is someone who was trained by and followed Elijah. The question is, was Elisha a first or second-generation prophet? The way I define it, he was most definitely a first-generation prophet. Notice how he threw down his cloak at the Jordan River, saying, *"Where is the Lord God of Elijah?"* (2 Kings 2:14, NKJV) rather than "Where is Elijah of the Lord God?"—he wanted to encounter God for himself. Even being *like* Elijah was not enough for him. His request was to have a double portion of Elijah's spirit (2 Kings 2:9). (We often settle for doing a few percent of what someone has accomplished. Let's ask for more! If we ask for too little, our city, family, or world may pay the price. We can't afford to be second-generation.) Interestingly, God was a rewarder to Elisha for so diligently seeking Him. In his life, Elisha performed twice as many miracles as Elijah...minus one. Then, after his death, as they dropped a dead body into a burial pit, it fell upon the bones of Elisha and the dead man rose to life. Thus, the miracles became the number of Elijah's times two! [Note: The Midrash, an ancient Jewish biblical commentary, assigns eight miracles to Elijah, sixteen to Elisha.]

In Exodus we see God speaking to Moses, giving his people a chance to be first-generation:

"Although the whole earth is mine, you will be for me a kingdom of priests and a holy nation." (Exodus 19:5-6)

However, in what Bill Johnson describes as one of the saddest moments in the Bible, the people turned it down:

When the people saw the thunder and lightning and heard the trumpet and saw the mountain in smoke, they trembled with fear. They stayed at a distance and said to Moses, "Speak to us yourself and we will listen. But do not have God speak to us or we will die." (Exodus 20:18-19)

It's tragic that they didn't accept what was offered to them. Think of what they missed. The same thing is offered to us. Will we accept it, or settle just to listen to someone else who did accept the offer? We all need leaders, but the best leaders have this heart of Moses: *"I wish that all the Lord's people were prophets and that the Lord would put his Spirit on them!"* (Numbers 11:29), desiring that their people be first-generation.

In growing in our calling or in our walk with God, we always get the chance to be first-generation or second-generation. So, which are we? Are we riding on someone else's coattails, or do we want to pave the way ourselves? If we are not first-generation, we're missing out on the journey and excitement of a lifetime. Only in becoming first-generation will we find what it takes to move ahead in *our* day and age, rather than in the day and age of the person we are following.

Tips to Grow in our Curiosity, Seeking, Desiring, and Hunger

There are ways to grow in these things. First, ask God to show you what is off your grid—questions you don't even know you should be asking. When it does come onto your grid—when you discover it—seek it! Then desire it. Then have a hunger for it—and especially for God who created all things. Second, don't settle for second-generation anything. The fun is in finding it! The journey truly is as important as the destination. Third, when you teach, don't make it your goal only to impart information. Ignite a curiosity and hunger deep within people. It will drive them to more. (This applies to evangelism, too—leave people with a hunger to seek more of God on their own.) As this quote attributed to Antoine de Saint-Exupery says, "If you wish to build a ship, do not divide the men into teams and send them to the forest to cut wood. Instead, teach them to long for the vast and endless sea." In longing for the sea, they will be more than motivated to build the ship. Fourth, remember that curiosity and desire are highly valued by God. They are ways God draws us to Himself. There are many things He wants to show us and has given us curiosity to ask about. So, ask Him to speak to you. Fifth, look for other curious, hungry people, and seek God together for more. You will encourage each other when you share what you find.

Call to Him, and He will answer you and show you great and unsearchable things you do not know. There are no limits here, often no grid that these things fit on. We will discover all sorts of things: it may be what God is like; it may be how we are deeply loved and meaningful to Him; it may be what lies ahead; it may be how we are called to change the world. Or it may be something altogether different! As we seek Him, God will reward us. He loves us to be curious and in pursuit of Him. We were designed to be fascinated by One who is extraordinarily fascinating.

Part I

Time

2
God and Time

We tend to put God and His abilities in a box. That box needs to be blown apart every so often! Talking about God and time will do just that.

I'm going to start with some familiar verses that, once you start thinking about them, are baffling! Like twentieth century physics, which I will discuss momentarily, these show that God's experience of time is very different from our own. We will see that not only does physics reveal how time is different than we might think, but that Scripture also boggles our minds in this regard.

First consider these words of Peter:

With the Lord a day is like a thousand years, and a thousand years are like a day. (2 Peter 3:8)

Many times, we read this thinking it is God's version of, "Wow that day just flew by. Time flies when you are having a good time!" I don't think so—we cannot impose upon God our emotions about how fast our day felt. This verse is trying to get us to grasp that God's time is not our time. In creating the universe, He could do a million years' worth of work in what He sees as one day. And in one day He could answer the prayers of a million people, untangling problems that took years to make. There is always enough time in His day to help you. This section of Scripture shows that God's promises (Peter is talking about Jesus' return) are made from an eternal perspective; He sees the fulfillment as clearly as though it were tomorrow...it *is* coming! Yet, in our experience of time, it could be coming now, later, or at any moment. So, Peter is telling us to be patient and faith-filled.

Now consider this verse in Revelation:

> ***"I am the Alpha and the Omega, the First and the Last, the Beginning and the End." (Revelation 22:13)***

This is another verse we tend to skip over. However, what if I came to your house and told you that I was the beginning? That wouldn't make much sense, because usually the beginning of something is an *event*: the shot of a starting pistol, a declaration of war, some point on the calendar. Yet here Scripture is saying that a *person* is the beginning...and the end. That is mind-boggling. When Jesus was called the *Alpha* and the *Omega*, He was not just at one time the *Alpha* (the beginning) and at another time will be the *Omega* (the end) but is *simultaneously* the *Alpha* and the *Omega*. This again shows that God is outside of time.

Now consider these words Jesus spoke to the Pharisees, which probably were as mysterious to them as they are to us:

> ***"Before Abraham was, I am!" (John 8:58, KJV)***

I love this verse because it is combining the past tense (*was*) with something that is timeless (*am*). It is connecting our time frame to God's. Those verb tenses would not make sense unless they were talking about transcending time. This saying infuriated the Pharisees because they knew Jesus was calling Himself the "I Am" (or *Yahweh*), God's covenant name. That name itself is profound. The description "I Am" is saying that God is pure existence—pure actuality. For God, who is outside of time as we know it, who is talking to humans locked into time and space, could there be a better way to explain who He is? Yet for those of us confined by time, it is still difficult to fully wrap our minds around this concept.

Finally, here is a verse that admits God's timelessness is difficult to fathom:

> **He has made everything beautiful in its time. He has also set eternity in the human heart; yet no one can fathom what God has done from beginning to end. (Ecclesiastes 3:11)**

Although we enjoy the creation of our eternal God, and, although there is an eternal aspect within our very beings, we cannot mentally grasp His timeless existence and activities. However, that does not mean we should give up trying.

The Physics of Time

I now turn to the science of the past 120 years to ponder some thinking about time. Before 1900, it was just assumed that time marched on with everyone experiencing it the same way. Most would have assumed that God experiences time this way, too, were it not for radical verses like those above. In the late 1800s, most scientists felt that almost everything about the universe was understood, with a few loose ends to tie up that would complete our understanding. But in the 1900s, new theories and discoveries began unraveling man's confidence in his own understanding. This included what he thought about time.

In the early 1900s, Albert Einstein presented what is called the *Special Theory of Relativity*. One of the more shocking aspects of this, now experimentally verified, is that two people can experience time differently if they are moving at significantly different speeds. In his *General Theory of Relativity*, presented some years later, he found that time could also be experienced differently in a massive gravitational field.

Relativity asserts that if a person were to travel near the speed of light, his time would progress more slowly than ours. If he were to return to us, he would have indeed aged less than we had.

Consider this thought experiment: Suppose our twin brother travels just under the speed of light to visit Alpha Centauri (one of the nearest stars to the sun) some four light-years away. (A light-year is the distance light travels in one year, so it takes four years for light from Alpha Centauri to reach the earth. If our twin were traveling near the speed of light, it would take him about four years to get there and another four years to get back.) First let's look at what relativity says that we will see from our frame of reference on earth. It says that, if we could see our twin's watch, we would see that it, his heartbeat, and time itself had slowed down for him. He would also appear flatter to us and more massive. Also, events that appear simultaneous to us may not be to him. One of the strange things about relativity, however, is that he would think the same things about us! When our twin reaches Alpha Centauri and turns around, once again traveling near the speed of light, we would again think his time had slowed down. Because time had been slower for him, once he returned to earth, he may have only aged two months: one month going to Alpha Centauri and another month coming back. But we would have aged the full eight years!

Now let's look at the trip from our twin's point of view. During the period of acceleration, he would experience the stars in his direction of motion moving much closer to him: Alpha Centauri, starting at four light-years, may end up being only one light-month away. Once he reaches his final speed, everything in his spacecraft appears normal to him. When our twin reaches Alpha Centauri and decelerates, he could look back and see the distance to earth expanding from one light-month to four light-years. To him, the entire trip would have only taken one month. Coming back home, the strange flattening of the distance to earth would once again take place during acceleration. Upon decelerating when reaching the earth, the distance to Alpha Centauri would once again return to four light-years. Our twin would have experienced only aging two months, and he would explain this by the mysterious shortening of distance. We would agree with his young age, not because any distances had changed, but because, to us, our twin's time had slowed down. The end result is the same: the experience of time would have been radically different between us and our twin.

Shockingly, this shows us that time is not something that proceeds in the same way for everybody; people in different frames of reference may experience it differently. Time is not what we once thought it was. Perhaps expanding our minds in this way may make it easier to see that God might experience time differently, too, although that's what He has said in His Word all along.

So, what is time? Science now looks at it as a dimension, but we still don't really know what it is. It helps me to think of a book—which basically is just a long collection of words. When we read it, we, in a sense, impose time upon it: what we have read is the *past*, what we are reading is the *present*, and what we have yet to read is the *future*. Yet if we stand back from that book, it is just a long string of words. In our own world, of course, we cannot stand back from time in this way, but it appears that God can. One might ask, have the "words" in the future already been "written" by God, or is He (and are we) writing them as we all "read" together? I think it is the latter—our future is still being written—otherwise we would have no freedom of choice; God wants us to truly love Him, which can only be expressed when we have the freedom to choose to love or not to love. However, God still seems to have the ability to see both past and future.

This "standing back" and looking at the past, present, and future, as if it all exists together, is a fairly good analogy for how Scripture describes God and time. He is, after all, the Alpha and the Omega—simultaneously the beginning and the end. This makes His perspective of the world very different from our own.

Time in God's Realm

I should clarify that when I say the realm of God is "timeless," I am not implying there is no time there, meaning everything is frozen with nothing changing. Scripture indicates quite the opposite. It is a place of vibrant activity. (More about this in Chapter 8!) Rather, I am saying it is outside our *experience* of time. Because time is so different in God's realm, we really have no good word to describe it. I am using "timeless" not to mean a lack of time, but to convey His being outside of time as we know it and being unaffected by this world's time.

When it comes to talking about time, the New Testament takes advantage of two Greek words: *chronos* and *kairos*. The former pertains to chronological time, whereas the latter pertains to a significant, or opportune, time. Often in prophetic revelations, a prophet will see a significant event coming, although he or she will not know when in our time frame that event will occur. In other words, the revelation describes the *kairos* (something that is significant for us to know and opportune for our action), but the *chronos* is not yet revealed...we just know that it is coming. We may not always know the day and the hour of a coming event, but it still calls for our attention. Not all revelations are lacking in *chronos* (specifying a time), however. More than four hundred years before the birth of Jesus, for example, the Old Testament prophet Daniel recorded a revelation (Daniel 9:25-26) which predicted, to the year, the death of the Messiah! (See my book *The Amazing Word of God*, p. 20, for details.)

Another difference between God's realm and ours is that, when God speaks, His words do not fade away like the words we speak in the physical world. His words remain forever. As it says in Isaiah:

> *The grass withers and the flowers fall, but the word of our God endures forever. (Isaiah 40:8; see also 1 Peter 1:24-25)*

God and Time

This means that God's words never fade away—they are eternal and are etched forever in heaven. His words, like God Himself, are not affected by time. For us, the implications are remarkable—it means that His promises are as powerful today as when He first spoke them!

Interestingly, when it comes to our *own* words and deeds, even though they may fade from our own memories, God, by standing back from time, can see them perfectly, as though they occurred only moments ago. This makes amazing (and almost incomprehensible) the fact that, when He forgives our sins, He remembers them no more (Isaiah 43:25). They are removed as far as the east is from the west (Psalm 103:12). They are no longer in the "timeline" that He sees! This shows how complete His forgiveness is.

Timelessness in Old and New Testament Prophecy

It is fascinating, though probably not surprising, that as God's words were written into Scripture, His timeless perspective was captured in its pages. We will see this is evident in far more than just a few verses; its influence can be seen repeatedly in the way the Bible is written. Nowhere is this clearer than in the prophetic books of the Bible. Of course, the very fact that prophecies sometimes speak of the future demonstrates God's timelessness. But the way these prophecies are written reveals even more.

The Prophetic Writings of the Old Testament

In the prophetic books of the Old Testament, the prophets were able to peer into God's eternal realm, where the past, near future, and distant future are as clear as the present. Here, themes and truths are so interconnected that, when the prophets wrote down what they were seeing, the near and distant futures were often intertwined. For example, in Isaiah chapters 7-9, we see some verses speak of the near future, then some jump to the far future, then more jump back to the near future, etc. In the Old Testament, the near future often dealt with the coming end to Israel's captivity, and the far future spoke of the freedom Jesus would bring hundreds of years later. And often, an even more distant future would be intertwined: the final victory Jesus will bring at His second coming. This intertwining of time frames has sometimes made it difficult to understand just what a prophetic word is about. Sometimes a prophetic word even has applications pertaining to multiple time frames. For example, the prophet Isaiah spoke this:

> ***Therefore the redeemed of the LORD shall return, and come with singing unto Zion; and everlasting joy shall be upon their head. (Isaiah 51:11, KJV)***

The immediate fulfillment is the return of Israel from its captivity in Babylon. Yet it also is a foreshadowing of the redemption won for us in Jesus' first coming. And, at the same time, it is a picture of the joy that the redeemed will experience in His second coming. [Note: It is good not to *force* fulfillments upon a prophetic verse, saying, for example that it was intended to pertain to modern-day America. If you want to make parallels, that is fine; just be clear that is what you are doing. Here I am sticking with obvious applications, which is always a good approach to interpreting Scripture.]

Some have likened this to looking at mountain peaks. From a distance, two mountain peaks can look like one, but it is not until you drive past one of them that you can see that the other peak is much farther away than the first. The Old Testament prophets often bounced from one mountain peak to the other and back again, describing what they were seeing without distinguishing the actual sequence of events. For many of these prophecies, we are now at a time when we can tell one peak from the other, because one is past and the other ahead. In the prophet's day, however, the peaks blended together. The prophecies were written this way because the prophets stared upon the revelation of a timeless God.

The Prophetic Writings of the New Testament

It would be surprising if we did not see this same "timeless" aspect in the prophecies of the New Testament. The largest of these prophecies are in Matthew 24 and the book of Revelation. Since both involve future prophecies (future with respect to the time they were written), there have been diverse interpretations of both (often with heated debates).

Matthew 24 (and its parallels in Mark 13 and Luke 21) contains two parts: Jesus' prediction of the fall of Jerusalem (Matthew 24:1-28) and the signs leading up to His second coming (Matthew 24:29-51). Many interpretations place both parts in the same time frame—they either see both as pertaining to our future, or they see both as being fulfilled by the fall of Jerusalem around AD 70 (which, when you compare the details of Matthew 24:1-28 with historical events, is a remarkable fit; also consider Jesus' words to the original hearers that it would occur in their generation). However, the interpretation which puts the entirety of Matthew 24 into the AD 70 time frame somehow must include what appears to be Jesus' second coming, which is not easy to explain.

Although Matthew 24 may appear like a seamless timeline, if we demand that both parts are in the same time frame, then we end up either ignoring history or having to explain that, in some sense, Jesus has already come again. It may be better to take the Old Testament model that both parts of Matthew 24 are warnings which will be fulfilled by two different times on earth.

Some might argue that the fall of Jerusalem in AD 70 was a *type* or *foretaste* (as will be discussed shortly) of another fulfillment of the fall of the temple which is yet to come, and therefore the entire prophecy can be thought of as coming in our future with a foretaste in AD 70. While that is possible, we may not know for some time whether that is the case (that is, whether the temple in Jerusalem will be rebuilt). Perhaps the best approach to Matthew 24 (and the book of Revelation) is to learn the lesson it is meant to convey, which sometimes seems to get lost when we argue about detailed roadmaps into the future.

Now to the book of Revelation. It is here where Jesus is called the *Alpha* and the *Omega*—the beginning and the end. This highlights His timelessness. The book shows that no matter what happens on earth, nothing will affect His timeless nature and mission. It is interesting how Revelation 12:12 shows that Satan is far inferior to God in this way, saying *"his time is short"*!

Once again, much debate has gone into how this book predicts future events. I am not sure I want to get into this debate, but I do want to point out some ways in which God's timelessness is displayed.

After the letters to the seven churches are presented in Revelation 1-3, chapter 4 begins a dramatic glimpse into heaven. In chapter 5, the call goes out for someone worthy to open the end-time scroll. The worthy one appears: the Lamb who was slain. This is tying the entire prophecy of Revelation to the most important event of all time: the sacrifice of Jesus. As significant events and the plans of God are about to be revealed, it is important to see that this sacrifice is the pinnacle event to which everything else is connected. To us, chapter 4 may seem like a disconnect in time with the rest of Revelation, but in heaven, the connection is solid and clear for all to see.

After this, pictures of events on heaven and earth are revealed (with the events in heaven affecting those on the earth). Amid these revelations, Revelation 12 comes along. This chapter gives us a prophetic revelation from a timeless point of view as it pulls back and shows us a timeline extending from ancient history to a time still in our future. It begins with the original rebellion of Satan, portrays the birth of Jesus, then paints a picture of the ensuing war between the two. It then widens the scope of this battle (in space and time) to involve all who follow Jesus. After Revelation 12, subsequent chapters focus once again on coming events in heaven and on earth, finally ending with our ultimate victory and the physical descent of heaven to earth.

Again, for many of the events described in Revelation, there is debate as to which of them have already happened and which are yet to come. Once again, it could be that some of the historical events which closely match the descriptions in Revelation are actually foretastes of other events yet to come. I don't know the answer to that, but I would be surprised if the Second Coming of Jesus, just as was the case for other major events of the Bible, did not have foretastes—events similar to and pointing toward what Scripture says will happen at the end of the age— perhaps even growing in intensity along the way.

Foretastes, Foretypes and Foreshocks

Another way we see God's timelessness is that, both in His Word and in life (as the Author of history), there are often **foretastes** of momentous events He is about to bring forth. These are glimpses, or tastes, of what is yet to come.

The death and resurrection of Jesus were the most momentous events in human history, and each had their foretastes in the times preceding them. Many Old Testament prophecies gave future glimpses of Jesus' death, sometimes involving the smallest of details. Isaiah 53 is perhaps the most notable example of this; it describes the suffering He would go through, and what it would accomplish. Psalm 22 is similar, foretelling how He would be pierced, and that lots would be cast for His garment.

There are hundreds of prophetic glimpses about Jesus in the Old Testament. The foretastes of His death and resurrection continue on in the New Testament, from signs at His birth (prophecies of His death) all the way to the raising of Lazarus (a foretaste of His resurrection). And His resurrection, Scripture says, is itself a firstfruit (or foretaste) of our own resurrection:

> **But Christ has indeed been raised from the dead, the firstfruits of those who have fallen asleep. (1 Corinthians 15:20)**

There are also *foretypes* (often just called *types* or *patterns*), which are historical events or people that are patterns of something or someone yet to come. In Romans 5:14, Adam is said to be a foretype of Jesus in that they both brought something to mankind (one sin and the other salvation). The story of Abraham's call to sacrifice his son Isaac (Genesis 22) is a remarkable foretype of the death of Jesus, which, in Abraham, we see from a father's perspective.

There are also occurrences that I would describe as *foreshocks*: Just as earthquakes have aftershocks, with God there are often foreshocks—startling events connected to things that lie ahead. At Jesus' death, when the price for our lives was paid, the resurrection-foretastes built into a crescendo, including this, a literal foreshock of the resurrection power to come:

> **And when Jesus had cried out again in a loud voice, he gave up his spirit. At that moment the curtain of the temple was torn in two from top to bottom. The earth shook, the rocks split and the tombs broke open. The bodies of many holy people who had died were raised to life. They came out of the tombs after Jesus' resurrection and went into the holy city and appeared to many people. (Matthew 27:50-53)**

When Jesus died and His blood dropped upon the ground, a wave of resurrection power was released. Even as a foreshock, it shook the earth and raised people from the dead. Jesus was raised a few days later. This wave of God's power that shook the earth is not done shaking yet. It is a timeless phenomenon released upon the earth, continuing to have miraculous manifestations and bringing people new lives. And one day that same power will raise *our* mortal bodies, living or dead, transforming them from one type to quite another (1 Corinthians 15:51-52).

Bookends

Sometimes God orders human history as though He were writing the beginning of a chapter with the end in mind. The beginning can contain foretastes of what is in the end. In these cases, the beginning and end become bookends to what lies in the middle. Such is a mark of God's authorship on the order of things.

For example, consider the life of God's Son. When Jesus was born, He was wrapped in swaddling cloths (Luke 2:7,12 NKJV). Swaddling cloths were long strips of linen wrapped tightly over a baby to make it feel secure. But why was attention given to this detail? At the end of Jesus' life, Scripture says this: *"Peter, however, got up and ran to the tomb. Bending over, he saw the strips of linen lying by themselves"* (Luke 24:12). Again, long strips of linen. Such detail, authored by God, serves as bookends to what He wants us to see. The timeless God, who at the beginning also sees the end, does things this way.

It is not surprising that the entire Bible—human history itself—would have such bookends, the beginning containing foretastes of what the end will look like. Consider this description of the Garden of Eden:

> **Now the LORD God had planted a garden in the east, in Eden; and there he put the man he had formed. And the LORD God made all kinds of trees grow out of the ground—trees that were pleasing to the eye and good for food. In the middle of the garden were the tree of life and the tree of the knowledge of good and evil. A river**

> *watering the garden flowed from Eden... Then the man and his wife heard the sound of the LORD God as He was walking in the garden. (Genesis 2:8-10, 3:8)*

Notice three things in these verses: a river, trees, and God's presence. That was the beginning of the Bible. Now look at the very last chapter, when the city of God will come upon the earth:

> *Then the angel showed me the river of the water of life, as clear as crystal, flowing from the throne of God and of the Lamb down the middle of the great street of the city. On each side of the river stood the tree of life, bearing twelve crops of fruit, yielding its fruit every month. And the leaves of the tree are for the healing of the nations.... There will be no more night. They will not need the light of a lamp or the light of the sun, for the Lord God will give them light. And they will reign for ever and ever. (Revelation 22:1-2,5)*

Again, we have a river, trees, and God's presence. These are bookends for human history, and for the Bible itself. This is the doing of the Alpha and the Omega, simultaneously the beginning, the end, and the in-between! The beauty that was in the beginning, which man lost, is like that of the end, which Jesus won back, with a remarkable story of redemption in between.

Therefore, we see that, not only are there verses that *say* God is outside of time as we know it, but that fact also is reflected in the very way His Word is written. For the Author of it is timeless. He is the beginning and the end.

The God of the universe loves us intensely and calls Himself our friend. However, to also know that He is outside of time changes the way we look at things. He knew you from your beginning, and you will be overwhelmed by His goodness for thousands upon thousands of years when you live in the place He has prepared for you. When it seems that time is running out, know this: to God, time is not an issue. He will come through for you. He can do a thousand days' worth of activity on your behalf in just one day. Do not fear...you are a friend of the Alpha and the Omega!

3
Walking in the Now and Not Yet

Could it be that something as unfathomable as the timelessness of God has any connection with who we, as mere finite beings, are? Amazingly, as we partner with God in ministry, it does. First, let's look at Jesus and His ministry.

When Jesus walked on this earth, He never ceased to be God, but He chose not to utilize His divine nature:

> **Who, being in very nature God, did not consider equality with God something to be used to his own advantage; rather, he made himself nothing by taking the very nature of a servant, being made in human likeness. (Philippians 2:6-7)**

Jesus did this for several reasons. First, to pay for our sins on the cross, He did not utilize His divine nature to escape its agony; He had to suffer as a man in order to redeem us (Hebrews 9:22). Second, He wanted to show us how to live our lives, such as how to choose God over sin, and needed to do this without the help of His own divinity. Third, He wanted to model how to partner with God, both in life and in ministry. Scripture shows how He partnered with both the Holy Spirit and the Father: after His baptism and temptation in the wilderness Jesus *"returned to Galilee in the power of the Spirit"* (Luke 4:14; see also verses 17-19); and Jesus said He only did what He saw His Father doing (John 5:19). Through His example, He showed us the way He wants *us* to partner with God. In ministry, He did this for His disciples in teaching them to pray for the sick, by first watching Him, then having them participate, and then sending them out to do it on their own (Luke 9:1-2, 10:1-9). To us He said that we will do *"even greater things"* than He (John 14:12). Therefore, Jesus is our model for life and for the way we minister, with no limitations on the possibility of things we might do.

In laying down His divine attributes and taking on the form of man, Jesus also laid down the attribute of being outside of time—He became subject to being locked into space and time the same way we are. However, as we will see shortly, that did not mean His ministry did not have a timeless aspect. And since ours is like His, our ministry has a timeless aspect, too, as difficult as that is to comprehend.

Heaven Touching Earth

As is mentioned in the last chapter, the entire Bible (and human history itself) has two remarkable bookends: the heaven-like description of the Garden of Eden and the description of heaven that will come upon the earth, as depicted at the end of the Bible. Recall that these were alike in many ways—both contained descriptions of a river, trees, and God's presence. Even more amazing, however, is that there is *another* account like this in the middle of the Bible, in the book of Ezekiel:

> **The man brought me back to the entrance to the temple, and I saw water coming out from under the threshold of the temple toward the east (for the temple faced east). The water was coming down from under the south side of the temple, south of the altar.... As the man went eastward with a measuring line in his hand, he measured off a thousand cubits and then led me through water that was ankle-deep. He measured off another thousand cubits and led me through water that was knee-deep. He measured off**

another thousand and led me through water that was up to the waist. He measured off another thousand, but now it was a river that I could not cross, because the water had risen and was deep enough to swim in—a river that no one could cross. He asked me, "Son of man, do you see this?" Then he led me back to the bank of the river. When I arrived there, I saw a great number of trees on each side of the river.... Fruit trees of all kinds will grow on both banks of the river. Their leaves will not wither, nor will their fruit fail. Every month they will bear fruit, because the water from the sanctuary flows to them. Their fruit will serve for food and their leaves for healing. (Ezekiel 47:1, 3-7, 12)

Again, we have a river, trees, and God's presence (here: the temple). It is a description of an outpouring of the Spirit upon the earth, getting deeper and deeper, bringing nourishment and healing. The very fact that this is so similar to the two bookends shows that this outpouring can be thought of as heaven experienced on the earth. It is not surprising that the Holy Spirit would bring with Him something like heaven, because it is God's presence that makes heaven the wonderful place that it is.

The primary application for Ezekiel 47 is the ministry of the kingdom of heaven, both in Jesus' day and in ours. See, for example, Jesus' description of rivers of living water flowing from those who believed in Him, as He spoke of the Holy Spirit:

"Whoever believes in me, as Scripture has said, rivers of living water will flow from within them." By this he meant the Spirit, whom those who believed in him were later to receive. (John 7:38-39)

The term *kingdom of God* (or *kingdom of heaven*) is mentioned over 100 times in the New Testament. It is God's rule and reign in the hearts and minds of people. Jesus' words described the kingdom; His works demonstrated it. Just as the kingdom of the enemy is characterized by darkness, deceit, disease, destruction, bondage, and death, the kingdom of God is characterized by light, truth, healing, growth, freedom, and life. When Jesus came, He brought the kingdom as a heavenly invasion, obliterating the kingdom of darkness wherever the two met. Disease was replaced by healing, bondage by freedom, and death by life. His works showed that the kingdom of God is here and that it is good.

Some might ask, was this kingdom Jesus spoke about referring to the present or the future? Some verses speak of it as being now: *"Heal the sick who are there and tell them, 'The kingdom of God has come near to you.'"* (Luke 10:9). Others speak of it as coming in the future: *"I say to you that many will come from the east and the west, and will take their places at the feast with Abraham, Isaac and Jacob in the kingdom of heaven"* (Matthew 8:11). Therefore, as theologian George Eldon Ladd often said, it is *both* now and not yet!

The ministry of Jesus, therefore, can be thought of as the future invading the present—where foreshocks of the not-yet are made manifest in the now. Jesus, the *Alpha* and the *Omega*, was calling upon the *Omega* (heaven) to be manifest now. It is heaven invading earth!

When His disciples asked Jesus to teach them to pray, He said to pray like this: *"Your kingdom come. Your will be done on earth as it is in heaven"* (Matthew 6:10, NKJV). This describes His own desire and ministry, that the future kingdom be demonstrated here and now—that heaven touch the earth. In teaching us this prayer, He was asking *us* to pray this into being.

This is what Ezekiel 47 is portraying: the flow of God's Spirit, ushering in His kingdom, being pictured as heaven pouring onto the earth. Although the fullness of heaven will come on the Last Day, in our day God wants to pour out heaven like a river. Whenever heaven touches the earth like this, the results can be striking. This was Jesus' ministry, and He wants us to experience the same flow of the kingdom in our day to show the reality and goodness of His reign.

Bringers of the Not-Yet into the Now

When Jesus was on earth, He led the heavenly invasion of God's kingdom. Now He has asked *us* to be the precipitators of the kingdom of God. In Luke 10:9, for example, He sent the seventy-two to heal the sick and, in doing so, to proclaim, *"The kingdom of God has come near you."*

In the Lord's Prayer, He is giving us the mandate and authority to pray that the kingdom break into our world. The phrases, *"Your kingdom come. Your will be done on earth as it is in heaven"* are actually in the imperative tense, as if we are speaking those things to be done: "Kingdom, come! Will as in heaven, be done!" I call it the *prophetic imperative*, prophesying these words into the heavens, establishing it as a reality on earth. We are ordained, as priests and ambassadors, to bring this to the world. We are carriers of God's authority to call the not-yet to come into the now. This is who we are.

To see what this looks like, look at the ministry of Jesus or of any of the disciples. They were callers of the kingdom. However, their lives were not always easy, and they carried humble, generous, tenacious, sacrificial hearts. This combination—of the power of the kingdom and hearts like these—touched the world, often confounding the wise; but such were the ones God loved to use to display His amazing kingdom. So, too, God will use us.

Today He is sending us, and as we go, we, too, will see the kingdom with its life and freedom burst onto the scene, crushing the effects of the enemy's reign of destruction. We don't know where or how it may burst out next, but it is its nature to do so.

We, with Jesus at our side, are now point men and women in the heavenly invasion as we bring His authority and presence into our land.

In the previous chapter, we explored a fascinating aspect of God's character: His timelessness. It is perhaps not surprising that timelessness characterized the ministry of Jesus. But it is overwhelming, yet true, that Jesus has called us to this very same ministry; and it is the same not-yet-and-now characteristic that He is calling *us* to employ in order to bring His kingdom to the earth! He is calling us to be "Bringers of the Not Yet"—bringers of the future light, truth, healing, freedom, and life that are part of heaven's kingdom—to the earth today.

Walking with a Forward Gaze

What does timelessness mean for us in our everyday walks? How do we live in the now and also in the not-yet? To do this, our gaze must be forward. As Paul told the Philippians:

> ***One thing I do: Forgetting what is behind and straining toward what is ahead, I press on toward the goal to win the prize for which God has called me heavenward in Christ Jesus. (Philippians 3:13-14)***

The book of Isaiah says something similar:

> **"Forget the former things; do not dwell on the past. See, I am doing a new thing! Now it springs up; do you not perceive it? I am making a way in the wilderness and streams in the wasteland." (Isaiah 43:18-19)**

Before I say what I mean by this, let me say what I don't mean. First, I don't mean that we shouldn't look backwards to the cross and all that it accomplished. The cross is essential to keeping our lives centered. Even though it happened in the past, it is one of those timeless things that overarches all we are and ever will be. Second, I don't mean that we should simply ignore our hurts of the past and not seek healing for them. Sweeping them under the rug will keep us in our hurts and prevent us from going forward. God wants to heal us so that we can fully look forward. Third, I don't mean that we should ignore the past without having reflected upon it to learn any lessons it might be teaching us. Perhaps it is showing us how to do things better or how we need to change—and God's amazing, forgiving, life-changing presence will gladly bring this about. Having done this, however, we must not dwell on past failures, which God doesn't even remember! Our gaze must no longer be on the past, nor on ourselves. We must look forward, seeing the future God has destined for us.

If you have ever tried to walk or drive a car by only looking where you have been, you would have been in for a very strange ride! Looking forward gives us stability and a sense of direction. How often, however, do we try to go forward yet end up looking behind, our hands flailing away at memories of the past, entangled in thoughts of how we have fallen short, sinned, or been the victims of life? No wonder it is hard to go forward. Paul speaks to this very thing:

Therefore I do not run like a man running aimlessly; I do not fight like a man beating the air. *(1 Corinthians 9:26, NIV©1984)*

Here, in 1 Corinthians 9:24-27, Paul is comparing our life in the Lord with that of an athlete, whose focus is forward upon the prize. They go through training, steered by a focus on where they are heading. So, too, our looking to the not-yet gives us focus, confidence, and direction. And, when we are looking at the not-yet, we know one of our calls is to bring that not-yet into the now.

Erwin Raphael McManus, in his book *The Way of the Warrior*, speaks of Elijah hearing a future sound—one yet to come:

"There is the sound of a heavy rain" (1 Kings 18:41). Elijah's focus was upon the future, hearing something in the spirit that was not yet heard in the natural. McManus points out that we, too, need a perspective like this as we encounter each day, prophetically seeing and speaking to what is coming before it arrives (pp. 174-177).

God wants us free and confident that He is totally for us, is completely pleased with us, and has poured into us His life which is waiting to spill over into a world that so desperately needs it. In coming to the Lord, we are living in a new place, a place that gives us a fresh start every day. It renews our life with mercy, permeates us with God's Spirit, and sets our eyes upon a new horizon: the not-yet that is coming into the now—and we are part of its coming.

Citizens of a New Land

We are citizens of a new land:

> *But our citizenship is in heaven.* **(Philippians 3:20)**

We were placed in this world; however, we dwell in it as ambassadors, prophets, and priests of the new land (2 Cor. 5:20, 1 Peter 2:9, Revelation 1:6). That is our true identity. Knowing this changes everything. If the temptations of this world try to entangle us, we remind ourselves that we belong to another land. If people deride us in this world, we know that we are honored in the land to which we belong. As members of that new land, we are bestowed an authority which some in the world will recognize and others not, yet it is very real. We are callers of the not-yet into the now. We are vocalizers of God's words. We are demonstrators of the works of the King, showing that He is here, He is real, He is breathtakingly powerful, and He is very good.

As we walk in both the now and not-yet, we are sanctioned to call the not-yet into the now. We are authorized to bring the kingdom of God to the world, offering healing, freedom, and newness of life. Empowered with authority—like prophets with their staffs in their hands—we thrust our staffs into the ground saying, "Kingdom of God, come!" and then watch as His kingdom bursts onto the scene. This is who we are called to be. Our call and ministry are timeless!

Part II

Space

4
God and Space

In this chapter I'm going to jump right into physics. I begin with a look at the dimensions of space.

The Dimensions of Space

Besides time, which is often treated as a dimension, we live in a world of three dimensions: length, width, and height. In the late twentieth century, scientists began exploring the idea that particles may be vibrating ever so slightly into even more dimensions. Mathematical analysis suggested that if there were six or seven more dimensions than the three we are familiar with, it could explain why the fundamental building blocks of the universe are the way they are.

To comprehend additional dimensions, consider a world where there are only two dimensions. Picture, for example, two-dimensional beings living on a tabletop. They could not go above or below the table, nor would they know about anything that existed outside the plane of the table. If you were to set a cup on that table, they would experience it as a circle, only knowing where the cup and table met. We would know there is a world bigger than theirs. However, they would only know about us if we were to touch the table. Deciding to press our finger onto the table's surface, they would experience the sudden presence of an oval growing to about half an inch in diameter. That is what we would be like to them. If we laid a rubber band on a table, they would see the outside of it. However, living in three dimensions, we would be able to turn the rubber band inside out, and suddenly they would see what used to be the inside of the rubber band now on the outside.

Similarly, if something living in four dimensions came into our world, it could appear and disappear, and we would only see the piece of it that intersected with our three dimensions. Like the rubber band, it could take a basketball into its additional dimension and turn it inside out without destroying the ball.

After Jesus rose from the dead, He was able to appear and disappear. This may make us wonder if God lives in another dimension and is able to walk into our dimensions in a way similar to our touching the two-dimensional world on the tabletop. Personally, I don't think God's realm merely consists of other dimensions...I think it is more profound than that. I don't think God lives *within* dimensions; I think He *made* dimensions. I say this mainly due to His awesomeness. Interestingly, however, physicists now think that spatial dimensions, and even time as we know it, came into existence at the creation of the universe, which supports the view that the dimensions are part of God's creation. (See 1 Corinthians 2:7 with the interesting phrase: *"before time began."*) That begs the question: in what realm might God exist if not in another dimension? To delve deeper into all of this, I'd like to present another piece of recent physics that may be even more mind-boggling than what we have discussed so far. It is a phenomenon called *quantum entanglement*.

Quantum Entanglement

Besides relativity, another theory that revolutionized physics in the early 1900s was *quantum mechanics*. For the most part, the realm of quantum mechanics is at the subatomic level. However, its premises are easily verifiable in our laboratories. One of those premises is that small particles such as electrons do not have a fixed position but can be found anywhere their accompanying "probability cloud" says they might be. That probability cloud is wave-like in nature. Light exhibits wave properties when it passes through two adjacent slits in a piece of film and forms a diffraction pattern on a screen a distance away. (For this to happen, the wave must pass through both slits.) However, the same thing can happen with a beam of electrons! It is as though both slits come into play even though the point-like electron will only pass through one slit or the other, not both. As long as you don't know exactly where they are, electrons behave like waves. However, if you were to employ a detector telling you which slit the electron were to pass through, then the act of knowing this information destroys the wave-like diffraction pattern, and the electrons behave as if they were particles and not waves. Our knowing (or detecting) something changes its behavior!

Quantum mechanics can be applied to another situation where the results are even more bizarre. This phenomenon is called *quantum entanglement*. First, a little background: Electrons never stop spinning (they have a set amount of angular momentum). And, if they never interact with anything, they will always spin the same way. If there is a sufficient amount of energy, an electron can be created out of nothing, but its antiparticle, the positron, is always created at the same time. The positron's charge is opposite that of the electron, and when it and the electron are created, their two spins will be equal and opposite (if what created them had no net spin). Quantum mechanics will dictate that we don't know which way either of them is spinning, but we do know that their spins will always be opposite of one another.

If we were to create an electron-positron pair like this, we could separate them by great distances. Perhaps one might be here on earth and the other four light-years away. We still do not know what their spins are, but we do know they are opposite. Here is the strange thing: If we were to detect the spin of the electron here on earth, instantaneously we would determine the spin of the positron four light-years away and it would behave differently than it did before we knew its spin. In other words, if someone four light-years away were to do an experiment involving that very positron, the results would be different depending on whether we knew the spin of our electron here on earth. Thus, doing something here can have an instantaneous effect on something a vast distance away. This happens because the two particles are *quantum entangled*.

This result (which has also been experimentally verified) flies in the face of the circa-1900 view of the universe. (It is even unexpected if you bring in relativity theory, which is why Einstein struggled so much with this.) When quantum entanglement entered the scene, the universe suddenly violated the picture of particles neatly moving in three dimensions, only interacting with other particles, waves, or forces in their immediate vicinity. Suddenly the very act of knowing something could affect another part of the universe. Quantum entanglement says that there can be a connection between one particle and another particle (one *specific* particle of the vast number of particles that exist) somewhere else in the universe, and that connection has nothing to do with space.

To understand this more fully, let's say the universe were a gigantic pool table and quantum mechanics applied to the pool balls. Standing at one end of the table, we would think that a ball on the other end of the table would move only when another ball struck it. But quantum entanglement is saying that something can happen to a ball on the other end of the table without anything striking it! In fact, it can happen by our just looking at, or knowing about, a ball on our end of the table! Why would our *knowing* something affect something else?! And how could two specific pool balls be connected independent of where they are in space? It is as if *thought* entered the picture, which somehow could impact the world in a significant way.

This striking result caused some to think that the universe might be the result of some cosmic mental or computer-driven process, much like the simulation depicted in the movie *The*

Matrix. If you have ever seen a virtual-reality computer program, it simulates things happening in 3-dimensional space, even though that "space" does not really exist but rather is a product of the simulation. Similarly, some think the 3-dimensional space in which we live may be the product of a similar process on a cosmic level. Some have even gone so far as to think the universe is a computer simulation created by aliens. (If so, I know who that "alien" is!) There have even been some who have dreamed up tests to see if the universe is actually a simulation by a gigantic computer that digitizes space (much like a television screen simulates a picture by dividing it into a certain number of pixels). Most think that we don't see such "digitization," so if the universe really is a "simulation," the "computer" must be so amazing it is beyond our comprehension.

This brings us to the question: Is the universe all within the mind of God? As we stare into space on a starry night, are we looking at something that is in His mind? We know we are looking at His handiwork, which shows His enormity and creativity, but are the universe and its dimensions all *within* His mind, or are these a separate construct? Restating the question: Where are space and the universe in relation to God? I will first look into what Scripture has to say about God and space.

God and Space in Scripture

Scripture tells us that God made the universe (Genesis 1). God is infinitely creative, with all He formed displaying profound beauty. But what, or where, is the *canvas* upon which He created the universe? Scripture does not say exactly what (or where) the universe *is* except for within a few verses, such as these fascinating words of Paul:

> *For in him we live and move and have our being. (Acts 17:28)*

This is saying that the place we live, the way we move, and our very existence are all *in God*. We *live* in God. We *move* in God. Movement involves spatial dimensions and time, so this verse says that these, too, are in God. We have our *being* in God, meaning that our existence at every level—physical, mental, and spiritual—is in God. This is beyond being *created* by God, although that is certainly true; we actually *live within* Him. For me, this truth is at the same time fascinating, almost incomprehensible, and comforting. For those who know Him, it provides a feeling of safety and well-being. As Paul also said,

> *For I am convinced that neither death nor life, neither angels nor demons, neither the present nor the future, nor any powers, neither height nor depth, nor anything else in all creation, will be able to separate us from the love of God that is in Christ Jesus our Lord. (Romans 8:38-39)*

It is interesting how this speaks both of time (present and future) and space (height and depth), neither of which can separate us from God or His love. For we are in Him, and once love is established between us, nothing can tear us apart.

Like the verse in Acts 17 quoted above, Colossians states:

> *For in him all things were created: things in heaven and on earth, visible and invisible, whether thrones or powers or rulers or authorities; all things have been created through him and for him. He is before all things, and in him all things hold together. (Colossians 1:16-17)*

Again, this says that everything was created *in Him*. Also, *in Him* all things are *held together* (from the Greek word *sunistemi* which means "have their place" or "continue to exist"), which denotes a continued dependence of everything's existence on being within Him.

The Bible says other things about God and space. A theological principle dealing with God and space is His **omnipresence** (being everywhere), which is found in various places in Scripture. For example, in Jeremiah 23:24 we read, *"Do not I fill heaven and earth?' declares the Lord."* This is overwhelming considering the size of the universe. Each star is mind-bogglingly massive—our sun weighs a thousand trillion trillion tons. Our galaxy alone contains 250 billion stars. And there are about 100 billion galaxies in the universe. At the small scale, things are equally astounding. Our body contains 37 trillion cells, and each cell contains 100 trillion atoms. God knows it all. He knows what is happening today in the Andromeda galaxy, although light from its stars will not reach earth for 2.5 million years. And He knows what is happening within each of our cells, aware of its molecular structure which allows it to do the amazing things it does. The beauty, intricacy, and creativity found throughout the universe is dazzling, whether we are looking at the level of atoms, cells, human beings, waterfalls, solar systems, or galaxies. His fingerprints are on it all.

There are also verses in the Bible that show space being **transcended**. As mentioned earlier, Jesus, after His resurrection, was able to disappear and reappear (Luke 24:30-31, 36-39). Philip was translated from one place to another (Acts 8:39-40). And Old Testament prophets were sometimes privy to things that took place a great distance away (2 Kings 6:12). These are beyond our simple view of space!

Heaven, like earth, has spatial dimensions. See, for example, Revelation 21:15-17, which speaks of the length, width, and height of the city of God. Like our universe, heaven is a creation of God. It was also created with some form of time (Revelation 8:1: *"There was silence in heaven for about half an hour"*). Although heaven may have a different sense of time than we do, somehow its time and space will mesh with ours when heaven comes to earth (see Revelation 21-22). Because heaven is a creation of God, however, God exists even beyond it, as Solomon said when building his temple:

> *"But will God really dwell on earth? The heavens, even the highest heaven, cannot contain you. How much less this temple I have built!"* (1 Kings 8:27)

Heaven, which is even more awesome than earth, still does not contain the entirety of His being...*He* contains *it*. So, even though heaven is one of God's realms, the realm of His existence is even bigger. [Note: This verse can pertain both to heaven and to the universe, since the word "heavens" includes the earthly realm proceeding to the spiritual realms above that. So, God is bigger than them all.]

Where is Space?

Now we return to the question posed earlier: Where is the universe—space as we know it—in relation to God? Is space inside, outside, or alongside God? Some have the notion that God is somewhere within the dimensions of our world (maybe somewhere in space), and from there He created it. As shown above in 1 Kings 8:27, however, God is bigger than that. The universe is in *Him*.

What about the idea that God dwells in another dimension? As I said before, I don't think God lives *within* dimensions; I think God *made* dimensions. Even if there are other inhabitable dimensions, He would have to be bigger than them, too, in order for all things to be in Him. Also, science is revealing that time and the spatial dimensions came into existence when the universe was birthed. (That makes creation even more astounding!) This begs the question: What was outside not only the universe, but also space and time, that caused them to appear? It is a question worth pondering—with a surprisingly loving answer. Again, this demonstrates that God is outside of it all.

I also spoke earlier of the idea of the universe being a "simulation" like in the movie *The Matrix*. This may be closer to the truth. However, I don't think God created some sort of computer in which the simulation runs; it would make more sense that it runs in His unfathomably amazing mind as He tracks the motion of every particle in the universe—seeing, knowing, and sustaining things from the smallest to the grandest of scales. [Note: I use the notion of the mind of God loosely in this chapter, referring to His thought process—not trying to delineate His being. God is so incomprehensible to us that I can only rely on what Scripture says about His thoughts, will, emotions, and omniscience. See Isaiah 55:8-9, Psalm 147:4-5.]

We are getting so far outside of our realm of experience here that it is nearly impossible to conceive of how all this works. Nevertheless, Scripture does make certain things clear: We, and everything else, are in Him. The implications of this, when you think about them, are profound!

The name of God, *I Am*, shows that God *is*. So, in a sense, that which is within Him also *is*. The universe is a reality, and so is heaven. But both, at every level, are in Him and are subject to whatever He sets His mind to do (see Revelation 4:11). So, to change anything in this universe is, to Him, as simple as changing His mind about how it should be. He has set His mind to make the universe orderly and subject to the laws He has set in motion (Job 38:33). But He also has higher priorities that sometimes will violate those physical laws. (I will visit that subject in the last chapter of this book.)

So, what difference should this make in our walk and ministry with God? Everyone agrees that He is all-powerful (Luke 1:37, Job 42:2), so my picture of His ability to change circumstances being as easy as changing His mind should be nothing new.

However, many still have the notion that it is easy for Him to heal a headache but much harder to restore a blind eye. These are equally do-able for Him! Redirecting an oncoming tornado is no more difficult for Him than giving us peace about some issue. On His side of things, all of these are equally easy. What we ask of Him and our expectancy are what may be limited (James 5:13-18). We need to keep the limitations of our minds out of the picture and simply look to Him. We need to partner with Him, having the mindset that everything is possible and that He loves to display His goodness. Then we would be in for a radical adventure, as He shows us how His kingdom can affect the earth. We have God as our friend, whose power is unfathomable and whose creativity and ability to change things are limitless. And He is on a mission to love and pull people safely into His kingdom, even if it means bending the laws of space and time to do so. As we embark on this mission with Him, we may see Him do just that!

5
Walking in God's Presence

The previous chapter dealt with where the universe is in relation to God. This chapter deals with where God is in relation to the universe. This isn't an academic exercise—it is vitally important to pursue God, which is key to our growing in relationship with Him. There is nothing like His presence. But where is He to be found?

Some might approach this question with this world's understanding of space: Something is either in a place or it is not, so they feel that way about God—His presence is either in a place or it is not (which might be the case if He were coming in from another dimension). Others, knowing God is omnipresent, feel He is always here (and they are right), but leave it at that and don't really have an expectation of encountering His presence in another way. Scripture, however, paints a different picture of this. Especially when referring to the Holy Spirit, it speaks of varying levels of His presence, some being more tangible than others.

One attribute of God's presence is described by the Hebrew word *kavod,* which is translated *glory.* For example, 2 Chronicles 5:14 says that *"the glory of the LORD filled the temple."* Literally *kavod* means *heaviness* or *weightiness* (but also connotes God's beauty, awe, and excellence), showing that it is something that may be felt. As in 2 Chronicles 5:14, this manifestation of God's presence can fill a room. It can also rest on a person or an entire group. This is something beyond God's omnipresence—in the

Bible, it was only experienced in certain places and occasions. And as we look at the Scriptures, we will find that there is even more to be said about encountering God.

Levels of God's Presence

Sometimes when we talk about the presence of God coming, it brings a very good question to people's minds: Isn't God everywhere all the time? How can I use the phrase "when God comes" if He is already here? The reason is found when we look at the verses in Scripture that describe God being in a place. These verses show that there are various intensities, or levels, of God's presence.

1. God is Everywhere

The first level of God's presence acknowledges that God is everywhere all the time. In other words, He is *omnipresent*. For example, Psalm 139 says:

> ***Where can I go from your Spirit? Where can I flee from Your presence? If I go up to the heavens, you are there; if I make my bed in the depths, you are there. If I rise on the wings of the dawn, if I settle on the far side of the sea, even there your hand will guide me, your right hand will hold me fast. (Psalm 139:7-10)***

David is saying that no matter where we go, God's presence is there. This is very comforting, because we may find ourselves in places where we are really glad He is with us! And He is. He is always there.

[Note: As mentioned in the last chapter, science has found that there can be a connection between a particle and exactly one other particle somewhere in the vast universe. So, is it hard to imagine that no matter where you are, God knows exactly where to find you?]

2. God Indwells Believers in a Special Way

In the Gospel of John, Jesus describes another level of His presence: His *indwelling* presence. This second level is special for believers in Jesus. Jesus spoke of Himself, the Father, and the Holy Spirit as dwelling with us and in us:

> *"On that day you will realize that I am in my Father, and you are in me, and I am in you."*
> *(John 14:20)*

This is an amazing, mind-boggling reality: Jesus—yes, God Himself—dwells within us! We are people of His Presence. And the more we learn about how awesome God is, the more staggering His dwelling within us becomes.

3. God Comes More Intensely at Times

There are some Scriptures that describe yet another level: when God's presence comes more intensely at times, usually for a particular purpose. One example is found in the Gospel of Luke:

> *Now it happened on a certain day, as He was teaching, that there were Pharisees and teachers of the law sitting by, who had come out of every town of Galilee, Judea, and Jerusalem. And the power of the Lord was present to heal them.*
> *(Luke 5:17, NKJV)*

This shows that God was doing something unusual—an extraordinary level of His presence was there for a particular purpose, in this verse: to heal. Another example of this is found in Psalm 22:3, which says that God inhabits (in Hebrew: *yasab*) the praises of His people. Often during worship an awareness of God's presence comes; He is there in a way that is different from before. At such times I have seen even unbelievers weep, feeling something—a closeness to God—that they have never felt until then.

4. God's Overwhelming Presence

Some Scriptures describe a level of God's presence that is *overwhelming*—more than a human being can handle. When His presence comes with such intensity, a person is undone—physically, emotionally, or both.

In his book, *When the Spirit Comes with Power*, John White writes about people, both in Scripture and recent history, experiencing God at various levels. At the level of His overwhelming presence, sometimes words cannot describe the emotional shock of experiencing God's reality and holiness. White describes an experience that he himself had as "both terrifying and full of glory" while he was in worship (pp. 87-88).

Moses encountered this as well. When he spoke of meeting the Lord on Mount Sinai, the attitude of the people was, in essence, "If we go up the mountain where His presence dwells, we will be killed" (see Exodus 20:19). They were not exaggerating or misinformed. Moses alone approached God because he was desperate to know Him. God loves that desperation. God responds to the determination that, even if His presence were to kill us, we want Him so badly that we will go anyway. When Moses asked to see God's presence, God had to shield him from His fullness in the cleft of a rock so that he would not die, saying, *"you cannot see my face, for no one may see me and live"* (Exodus 33:20). Even this did not stop Moses from pursuing more, however. Later God said of Moses, *"with him I speak face to face...he sees the form of the LORD."* (Numbers 12:8). Moses had a heart to see Him. God truly is a rewarder of those who diligently seek Him (Hebrews 11:6, NKJV).

Another example of how a person can be physically overwhelmed by God's presence is this experience of Daniel:

> *And I heard a man's voice between the banks of the Ulai, who called and said, "Gabriel, make this man understand the vision." So he came near where I stood, and when He came, I was afraid and fell on my face; but He said to me, "Understand, son of man, that the vision refers to the time of the end." Now as He was speaking with me, I was in a deep sleep with my face to the ground; but He touched me, and stood me upright. (Daniel 8:16-18, NKJV)*

Even though the speaker in this passage was not actually God, but an angel, the presence of the Lord (and the vision) was so intense that Daniel fell to the ground like a dead man. Daniel couldn't move until the angel came and touched him. The aftermath of this incident is described a few verses later:

> *And I, Daniel, fainted and was sick for days; afterward I arose, and went about the king's business. I was astonished by the vision, but no one understood it. (Daniel 8:27, NKJV)*

Daniel was so undone that the physical effects of God's presence stayed with him for days after the encounter.

The book of Revelation offers another example of this intense level of God's presence. Here it is the apostle John talking—John who had known Jesus in the flesh for years. He was the disciple who was as close as a brother to Him, the one who put his head upon Jesus' breast at the Last Supper. But in Revelation 1, John says,

> *When I saw him, I fell at his feet as though dead. Then he placed his right hand on me and said: "Do not be afraid. I am the First and the Last." (Revelation 1:17)*

John had now encountered Jesus in His overwhelming glory, and its effect was pronounced.

There are more accounts of people being overwhelmed by the presence of the Lord. The Transfiguration (Matthew 17:6-7) and Paul's encounter with Jesus on the road to Damascus (Acts 9:1-9) describe such events. And 2 Chronicles 5:14 (KJV) speaks of the presence of the Lord filling the second temple to such an extent that the priests were no longer able to stand in order to minister.

There are times when we may encounter God at each of these levels. However, the boundary between them is not sharp. Sometimes we may experience a partially overwhelming presence of God through which we can actually live and perhaps not even faint, but it still may have effects on us.

God's Presence On Us and In Us

Jesus often spoke to His disciples about the Holy Spirit who one day would come upon them. This, of course, happened on the day of Pentecost:

> *When the day of Pentecost came, they were all together in one place. Suddenly a sound like the blowing of a violent wind came from heaven and filled the whole house where they were sitting. They saw what seemed to be tongues of fire that separated and came to rest on each of them. All of them were filled with the Holy Spirit and began to speak in other tongues as the Spirit enabled them. (Acts 2:1-4)*

As a result, many were added to the disciples' numbers. This was a fulfillment of Joel's prophecy that God was to pour His Spirit upon the earth (Acts 2:16-21). And it was a fulfillment of Jesus' words: *"But you will receive power when the Holy Spirit comes on you; and you will be my witnesses in Jerusalem, and*

Walking in God's Presence

in all Judea and Samaria, and to the ends of the earth" (Acts 1:8). Indeed, one is never the same again after receiving this encounter. To enable us to do all He asked, God has empowered us with His presence in this way. As people of His presence, however, we not only have Him *upon* us, but also *within* us, demonstrating the intimacy that we can have with the presence of God.

John 14 is perhaps the most detailed look into the inner working of the three Persons of God in all of Scripture. It's almost like peering into the Holy of Holies. In these verses, Jesus describes how intimately the Persons of the Trinity dwell with one another. Jesus is in the Father and the Father is in Him (verses 10-11, 20). The Holy Spirit is with the Father and the Spirit is the One whom the Father sends (verses 16-17, 26).

As a characteristic of this intimacy, the Persons of the Trinity honor and defer to one another. Jesus honors the Father: *"The Father is greater than I"* (verse 28). And in another place the Father honors the Son: *"You are my Son, whom I love; with you I am well pleased"* (Luke 3:22). Jesus honors the Holy Spirit, calling Him the *"Spirit of Truth"* (John 14:17), and the Holy Spirit honors Jesus, reminding us of everything Jesus has said (verse 26). This humility, honoring of one another, and love toward each other is a model of how we are to honor and love one another. It is an amazing depiction of unity and a stunning portrait of the interaction between the Persons of God. God values relationship.

What is also stunning, however, is how *we* are interspersed within these verses. As impossible as it may sound, *we* are a part of this intimate interaction within the Trinity! (This is even more extraordinary given what the Old Testament says is required to come near His presence…something that Jesus made possible by His sacrifice.) John 14 could not be a more remarkable depiction of how we, as believers in Jesus, have God living inside of us. First, in verse 17, the Spirit lives with us and will be in us. Then in verse 20, Jesus is in us and we in Him. Then in verse 23, Jesus and the Father will love us, come to us, and make their *home* in us. This is not just in heaven after we die, although it will be there, too. The context of these verses is what would happen soon, when Jesus would go to the Father (verse 12). The intimacy within the Trinity is astounding enough, but to find ourselves placed in their midst is almost too much to comprehend. That which the Persons of the Trinity give to one another—love, honor, and the enjoyment of being with one another—they give to us. We are deeply loved, honored, and enjoyed by God as we dwell in His awesome presence.

One might ask: Where does this intimate interaction between us and the three Persons of God occur? The answer is: everywhere we go. God is within us! One might also ask: Is God within us, or are we within God? The answer is: "Yes!" Both are correct, which seems almost impossible. But He who is not confined by space says this is true.

John 14 shows us how our life in the Lord involves closeness to Him. He is available to us all the time, whether we are coming to Him individually or collectively. It is also true that we, individually and collectively, can grow in this intimacy and in His anointing. We have Him completely, yet there is always more (Psalm 42:1). Just as more encounters with God were in store for the disciples who heard these words, more is in store for us. Such is life when we are close to the true and living God.

Experiencing God's Presence

How do we experience God's presence? Sometimes we just let Jesus' words, like those above, sink in and experience their reality. But other times we may encounter Him in the tangible, more intense levels I described at the beginning of this chapter. That is the way His presence is. Sometimes His presence is very apparent. In Acts 8, His presence was so obvious that Simon wanted to buy what he saw. Other times, He comes in a quiet way. In 1 Kings 19, Elijah found that God wasn't in the earthquake; He wasn't in the fire or in the whirlwind; He was in the whisper. Sometimes His presence is so subtle, it's almost like the touch of a butterfly wing. So, expect both.

What is it like when we experience God? (Here I will focus mostly on the Holy Spirit, since, in this life, that is how we usually encounter God's presence.) In both the New Testament Greek and the Old Testament Hebrew, the word for *Spirit* also means *breath* or *wind* (in Greek, *pneuma*; in Hebrew, *ruach*). He is so near, we share the same breath; He is something that fills us, as close as the air in our lungs. Yet, at the same time, He is a wind that is beyond us. He can be gentle, yet He can also blow down everything in His path. He is both intimate and awesome.

When the Holy Spirit comes, people's experiences today are quite similar to those recorded in Scripture. First, they often experience the fruit of the Spirit. They may feel a profound sense of love or the freedom of His joy. Perhaps, for the first time in their lives, they experience a true peace. People also experience the Spirit's gifts. That was certainly the case in the book of Acts.

God's presence often makes us aware of His nearness. We will do whatever it takes to be near to Him. It adds a new dimension to our worship. It can clear our minds, helping us focus on Him and letting us hear His voice more clearly.

The presence of God can also cause physical responses within us. It can be like an overloading of our nervous system—more than our physical beings can handle. People might tremble or shake (Jeremiah 5:22) or find it difficult to stand (Ezekiel 1:28); or they may feel sensations of warmth, heat, or electricity. Sometimes they feel like they are in a gentle rain. It is interesting that in Scripture, the effects of the Holy Spirit are often compared to the wind (John 3:8, Acts 2:2), rain (Hosea 6:3), or fire (1 Thessalonians 5:19, Acts 2:3). People's emotions can be piqued; they may weep easily or can't help but laugh. These responses can be deeply healing for people. There is often a profound story behind the outward appearance. If you see something strange, you may want to talk to the person afterwards before judging it by the way it looks. Also, don't worry if you don't feel anything unusual—that does not mean God is not there. I have seen lives radically transformed after not feeling anything physical during an experience with Him. (However, we can grow in our sensitivity to Him.) Each experience with God is different.

As an example of this, years ago we visited a place where God's presence was being poured out profoundly. After we got back, it was my Sunday to teach the school-aged kids. Everything started out normally—I had them run around for a while just to unload the adrenaline they carried at that age! At some point during the class, we prayed for God's presence to come, after which I could see that the kids were being impacted in a significant way. Our friends' son, Andy, a sweet boy with Down's Syndrome, was in the class. Normally he did not think abstractly, but I looked over at him and saw him in tears with his arms held out. He told us his arms were getting heavy because they were being loaded with all the years of teasing he had experienced from the neighborhood kids, and now God was removing that weight from his hands. The Spirit was so strong on these kids that we decided to take them into the main service to pray for the adults. That began a powerful move of God in our church, producing fruit that has endured even to this day.

Seeking More of God's Presence

In his exceptionally inspirational book, *Face to Face with God*, Bill Johnson points out that biblically, the activity of *seeking* is not passive. In other words, we don't seek God by just waiting around. For example, the Hebrew word for *waiting*, *qawa,* is translated "patiently waiting" in four of the times it is used, but in forty-nine other places it has the connotation of "writhing in pain as in childbirth" or "whirling in the air in dance." Johnson writes, "There's something about both the dance and giving birth that requires incredible resolve to reach an intended end. This is waiting patiently for God. It has intense focus, disciplined resolve, and a conviction that *nothing else will satisfy*. God is attracted to people who have that kind of tenacity and who are not satisfied with inferior things" (p. 121). Biblically, the word "wait" can also have the connotation of waiting as if setting up an ambush. Bill Johnson goes on to say, "It is almost militant, still carrying the discipline of the intense focus mentioned earlier, but along with an eager pursuit.... God is looking for someone who will get out of his or her routine and set up an ambush" (pp. 121-122, Bill Johnson, *Face to Face With God*, Lake Mary, FL: Charisma House, 2007, used by permission). That is the key; to pursue God, we must get out of our routines and do something different!

People with amazing stories of finding God usually began by seeking Him with desperate, passionate, tenacious, faith-filled hearts. We need those qualities, too, and can ask God for them. We also need focus. But where is it that we should set up an ambush?

We can and should seek Him individually, but finding other hungry people with whom to seek Him is also important and helpful. Also, try to find gatherings of people where the Holy Spirit is often present. Don't accept substitutes of those just going through the motions of what seemed to work years before. In whatever way you do find God's presence, stay in it a while and receive all He has for you, and ask for even more. One time I resolved that every time I felt His presence, I would stay in it twice as long as normal. That was a good decision! He rewards those who diligently seek Him.

Bringing God's Presence

Sometimes God just sovereignly "shows up" in a place or on a person...no one did anything special to bring it about. Often, however, since we are His sons and daughters in whom His presence lives, God gives us a role in bringing His presence to others. (See, for example, Acts 8:17; 19:6, John 7:38, and Isaiah 60:1-3.) Teachers at Bethel Church in Redding, California, use the analogy that, when it comes to God's presence, we are both thermometers and thermostats. We are "thermometers" in the sense that we can feel when God's presence is more intense. That is a good thing! But we are also "thermostats," because we can invite God to fill the place where we are. God responds to our invitation, and even *wants* us to invite Him (Luke 11:13). His presence can change the atmosphere, and when He comes, anything can happen!

It is important to bring the presence of the Lord wherever we go. When God's presence comes, even those who do not yet know Him can often sense and enjoy it, tasting that He is good. It can clear their minds of whatever is troubling them or standing in the way of God entering their lives. The works of the Lord that come with His presence (such as healing or prophetic words) can make them realize, "God is here, and He cares about me." All of this can make it far easier to lead people to the Lord.

God's Spirit is essential for ministry. We participate in His presence, power, and heart as we pray for others. Whatever it is we are doing in ministry is greatly enhanced by a higher level of His presence. It really is *His* ministry, and more of His presence means more things happen. With His presence, the words He wants to give people flow much more freely. With His presence, healing—and faith for healing—comes. One of the most productive healers of the twentieth century was Charles Price. It was said that if you could not find healing anywhere else, you should go to one of his meetings. Charles felt that when people tried to pump up their own faith, it was usually counterproductive. His premise was that when God's presence comes, faith comes, so he just asked God's presence to come during his meetings. The results spoke for themselves. There is nothing like the presence of God.

So how do we have more of God's presence when we minister? I find it best to start by asking Him to come. The Holy Spirit loves to come and loves to be welcomed. So I say, "Holy Spirit come" to invite my Friend to be here. Then I follow Him.

As previously mentioned, when the Holy Spirit comes, the atmosphere changes. The place becomes His. Usurpers—the enemy or his lies—lose their right to be there and must drop their chains on whomever we pray for. The Spirit's presence hovers over those who need healing, ready to heal anything out of alignment with God's perfect design. Encouragement comes. Words and anointing, which propel people into their God-given futures, are freely given by the Spirit. The kingdom shows up, glistening with the goodness of the King.

The presence of God changes things, whether it be among two people in prayer, an entire room full of people, a city, or a nation. We, the people of His presence, are indeed like thermostats, and have to collectively turn our "dials" so that more of Him might be made manifest. And in this way, though our King is always omnipresent, it will also be made known that He often dwells in a very tangible way—at locations on this earth, and in our very lives.

Part III

Matter

6
God and What Fills the Universe

The universe consists of more than space and time. It is also filled with substance, which we refer to as *matter*. But what is that, really? In this chapter I'm going to start with the Word and what it says about the beginning of the things that are in the universe.

The Beginning of Things in Scripture

According to the Word, the things of the universe had their beginning this way:

> *In the beginning God created the heavens and the earth. Now the earth was formless and empty, darkness was over the surface of the deep, and the Spirit of God was hovering over the waters. And God said, ... (Genesis 1:1-3)*

What is most clear is that the universe had a beginning and that God created it. It is not certain whether the second sentence (v. 2 and beyond) is speaking of the beginning of the planet earth or of the universe. Perhaps it applies to both. Should it apply to the universe, the words "formless" and "empty" (the latter can be translated *a chaotic void*) are interesting in that we know even space and time had no meaning before the universe began. Likewise, "surface" (or *face*) of the "deep" (which can denote a deep secrecy) is thought-provoking; might it be speaking about something in the mind of God? "Waters" (literally *face of the sea*), to me, denotes something immense that is about to flow. Everything was in a state of readiness, but it did not begin until God spoke.

The revivalist Reinhard Bonnke once said, "It struck me when I read Genesis 1, how the Holy Spirit was brooding over the chaos—in the strict darkness, brooding, hovering, hovering, brooding. Nothing happening. Absolutely nothing—until verse three. And then God said, 'Let there be light.' Suddenly I saw something I never saw before. The Holy Spirit waited for the word. He couldn't begin the miracle of creation without the spoken word." The hovering may have been going on for millions of years; we don't know. God chose that the spoken word is what gave the world its beginning. Bonnke went on to say how, in the same way, the spoken word is what births faith in people's hearts, something he has seen millions of times over as he ministered in Africa. Something important is connected with the speaking of things. What is that about?

As Reinhard Bonnke mentioned, speaking plays a part in salvation. Paul says that the vocalization of the word, which we hear ourselves speak, is part and parcel of entering into a saving relationship with God:

> *If you declare with your mouth, "Jesus is Lord," and believe in your heart that God raised him from the dead, you will be saved. For it is with your heart that you believe and are justified, and it is with your mouth that you profess your faith and are saved. (Romans 10:9-10)*

Other verses speak of the power of His voice, as well. Here are some remarkable examples:

> *Ascribe to the LORD, you heavenly beings, ascribe to the LORD glory and strength. Ascribe to the LORD the glory due his name; worship the*

LORD in the splendor of his holiness. The voice of the LORD is over the waters; the God of glory thunders, the LORD thunders over the mighty waters. The voice of the LORD is powerful; the voice of the LORD is majestic. The voice of the LORD breaks the cedars; the LORD breaks in pieces the cedars of Lebanon. He makes Lebanon leap like a calf, Sirion like a young wild ox. The voice of the LORD strikes with flashes of lightning. The voice of the LORD shakes the desert; the LORD shakes the Desert of Kadesh. The voice of the LORD twists the oaks and strips the forests bare. And in his temple all cry, "Glory!" (Psalm 29:1-9)

"My word that goes out from my mouth: It will not return to me empty, but will accomplish what I desire and achieve the purpose for which I sent it." (Isaiah 55:11)

For you have been born again, not of perishable seed, but of imperishable, through the living and enduring word of God. (1 Peter 1:23)

The spoken word of the Lord can shake the earth. It is endued with power. It is alive and will endure forever. Words, especially those of God, are important. They can be written, read, or contemplated in our minds. But God has made it so that something special goes on when they are vocalized. (For those who cannot speak or hear, God will use whatever way those individuals communicate to those around them. He hears it!) So, what is it about sound that God finds important enough to make it the beginning point of the universe? Looking at it scientifically, it is just vibrating air. Or is it?

The Sound of Music

Music, also vibrating air, also has a special place in Scripture—there are over 800 references to it! I've always been fascinated by the production of sound. Stringed instruments, such as guitars and violins, work because a vibrating string passes its vibrations to the instrument's body. As this vibrates, it causes the air inside of the instrument to vibrate as well. These vibrations travel to the air of the outside world where they eventually reach our ears, vibrating our ear drums and the tiny bones nearby. So, what is it about vibrating strings or vocal cords that are special to God?

First, God tells us to worship in song:

> *Speak to one another with psalms, hymns and spiritual songs. Sing and make music in your heart to the Lord. (Ephesians 5:19, NIV©1984)*

And this verse even speaks of God, Himself, singing:

> *The LORD thy God in the midst of thee is mighty; he will save, he will rejoice over thee with joy; he will rest in his love, he will joy over thee with singing. (Zephaniah 3:17, KJV)*

Other verses speak of the connection between music and God's presence, or between music and His doing something supernatural:

> *But thou art holy, O thou that inhabitest the praises of Israel. (Psalm 22:3, KJV)*

> *Elisha said... "But now bring me a harpist." While the harpist was playing, the hand of the LORD came on Elisha. (2 Kings 3:14-15)*

> *Whenever the spirit from God came on Saul, David would take his lyre and play. Then relief would come to Saul; he would feel better, and the evil spirit would leave him. (1 Samuel 16:23)*

> *After consulting the people, Jehoshaphat appointed men to sing to the LORD and to praise him for the splendor of his holiness as they went out at the head of the army, saying: "Give thanks to the LORD, for his love endures forever." As they began to sing and praise, the LORD set ambushes against the men of Ammon and Moab and Mount Seir who were invading Judah, and they were defeated. (2 Chronicles 20:21-22)*

There are many types of music mentioned in the Bible. The verses below show a variety of them, which once again shows that there is something about music that is important to God:

> **Sing joyfully** *[ranah: shout for joy]* **to the LORD, you righteous; it is fitting for the upright to praise** *[halel: demonstrative praise]* **him. Praise** *[yadah: praise with outstretched arms]* **the LORD with the harp; make music** *[zamar: make music in praise to God]* **to him on the ten-stringed lyre. Sing** *[shyr: sing, like a strolling minstrel]* **to him a new song; play** *[nagan: play, strike strings]* **skillfully, and shout** *[teruw: shout or blast a shofar]* **for joy.** *(Psalm 33:1-3)*

There are many parallels between our lives and music. I have found this especially true when ministering with a team, where our desire is to follow the Spirit's lead and to be open to whatever He wants to do and to whomever He wants to use. 1 Corinthians 14 talks about the *manifest presence of God*, which can be translated "the dancing hand of God." His hand can dance from person to person—it can be with you one moment and someone else the next. A ministry team is like an orchestra and the "dancing hand of God" the orchestra leader. As in an orchestra, each member needs humility and boldness—humility when it is someone else's turn to shine, boldness when the dancing hand of God rests upon you. When this all works as it should, it has a distinct beauty—a diversity of gifts playing in harmony.

I know this seems like following a rabbit trail when my initial purpose in this chapter was to examine matter and how it was created. So, let us get back to that and see where science has taken us in the pursuit to understand what fills the universe.

Matter throughout the Universe

Every atom is made up of electrons orbiting a nucleus. If the outer electrons were to receive energy, they might go into orbits beyond their normal orbital paths and then fall back where they should be. When this occurs, they give off light at a distinct frequency (that is, a distinct color). Every element has a distinct set of frequencies for the light they emit. Thus, by looking at the light from distant stars, we can tell exactly what elements they contain and how much of each one is present. Amazingly, when examining astronomical objects throughout the universe, astronomers have seen that the elements out there are the same as those we might find on earth. And since the frequency of light emitted also depends on the laws of physics and the numerical constants which are part of those laws, they have also found that the very same laws here on earth are exactly the same throughout the vast universe. So, everything throughout the universe is built with the same ingredients and obey the same laws that we know about here.

Even though the universe is built of the same building blocks found everywhere, the variety of things in the universe is astounding. The better telescopes we build, the more remarkable things we observe. Beautiful cosmic structures are uncovered that we never even dreamed existed. Even the sizes of things are astonishing. As big as the earth is, the sun is incomprehensibly bigger: 1.3 million earths could fit inside the sun. However, Arcturus, a star 37 light-years from earth, is so huge that 16,400 suns could fit inside of it. Betelgeuse, another star, is even bigger—38 times the diameter of Arcturus—so 870 million suns could fit inside of it. And the star UI Scuti is bigger yet—1.8 times the diameter of Betelgeuse—so 5 billion of our suns could fit inside of it! If this star were at the location of our sun, it would engulf not only the earth, but also Mars and Jupiter, and it would almost reach Saturn as well. Why would God create something so big? I think it's just because He could!

In regard to the mysteries of space, we can pose an interesting question: Does the Bible reveal any scientific facts that we know now, but that were not discovered at the time the Bible was written? Actually, it does! While some descriptions of the sun moving in relation to earth are poetic descriptions of what we see from our vantage point (such as the sun "going down" in Psalm 104:19), Job, perhaps the first book actually penned, speaks of how the earth floats in the vacuum of space: *"He spreads out the northern skies over empty space; he suspends the earth over nothing"* (Job 26:7). And speaking of stars all being different, we have this verse: *"The sun has one kind of splendor, the moon another and the stars another; and star differs from star in splendor"* (1 Corinthians 15:41). Science had not revealed any of these facts to the writer, but God had.

The Science of Matter

From early on, it has been the quest of science to understand matter and to see if it is made up of fundamental building blocks and, if so, what those building blocks are. One of the earliest attempts to do so was made by Empedocles (494-434 BC), who said that all matter is made of air, fire, earth, and water. As science progressed, it found that matter was actually made up of a variety of *elements*, such as hydrogen, carbon, and oxygen. Those elements, when combined in the right way, could make a huge variety of other substances, such as water. As time went on, more and more elements were discovered, eventually growing to more than one hundred. So, scientists began to wonder if something even more fundamental made up those elements. Indeed, electrons, protons, and neutrons were discovered which, in different combinations, make up the atoms of all the elements.

As particle accelerators were developed, other fundamental particles besides electrons, protons, and neutrons were discovered. Some were found to be relatively stable, such as positrons (antiparticles of electrons), muons (like electrons but much heavier, with a lifetime of 2.2 microseconds), and neutrinos (nearly massless particles having no electric charge, which can pass through vast amounts of matter without interacting). Others were not stable, meaning that they decayed into other particles after existing for a very short amount of time. As more and more of these were discovered, once again they ended up with over a hundred of these fundamental particles, and the quest to find even more fundamental building blocks began.

It was theorized (and later, experimentally verified) that particles such as protons and neutrons are actually made up of *quarks*. These unusual particles either come in sets of three (such as the three quarks in the proton and the neutron) or in quark-antiquark pairs. While most forces (such as the electric force between electrons and protons) decrease as the distance between the particles increases, making it possible to pull them apart, it is not so with the force between quarks. That force actually *increases* with distance. Therefore, it is impossible to separate the three quarks within a proton. (It is interesting that God created nature, at a fundamental level, to be built of inseparable sets of three—it sounds like the Trinity!)

The "truly" fundamental particles were then considered to be the quarks, leptons (which included electrons, muons, and neutrinos), and bosons (the mediators of forces, such as the photon). However, theorists again began speculating whether something even more fundamental might make up all of these.

One interesting theory that might explain these even smaller building blocks is called *string theory*, which hypothesizes that the fundamental particles are actually different modes of vibrations of vibrating energy strings. However, these vibrations would not just be into the three spatial dimensions we know about but, in order to account for all the particles, would vibrate into six or seven other dimensions as well.

I find it interesting, reflecting on how much the Word says about voice and music, that vibrating strings may lie at the root of all that exists in this universe. Maybe, in a fundamental way, we are made up of God's voice. Maybe we are made of music!

Michio Kaku, Professor of Theoretical Physics at the City University of New York, said this: "Just as a violin string's different vibrations produce different notes, energy strings' unique vibration patterns correspond to different subatomic particles. If this picture is correct, all of physics can be summarized as the harmonies of tiny vibrating strings, chemistry as the melodies of interacting strings, and the universe as a symphony of all strings resonating distinctly."

So, what are the things that we see in this world really made of? It's fascinating to think that when God spoke the universe into existence, the innermost substance of the things which were created were vibrations. It may be that His words which caused the universe to come into being did not fade away but resound within the very things that are in this world. It is fascinating, too, knowing God's interest in music that, in a sense, we are made of music. Perhaps Paul's admonition to live in harmony with one another (Romans 12:16) has a deeper analogy than we thought! There are many things in the world that we can resonate with. It seems that the world is trying to get us to dance to a variety of its drummers, not many of which are playing productive tunes. It is far better to dance to the beat of the One who created us—there is no sound like His. Let our lives be ones that resonate with worship unto the Lord!

A Far Sweeter Sound

There is a sound of heaven! (See Revelation 5:8-9, 14:2-3, 15:2-3.) I think that it is something that can be captured and heard upon the earth. The previous chapter mentioned the honor, love, and enjoyment that the Persons of God give to each other and to us (John 14). This is a "sound" that the world needs to hear. It stands in distinction to the disharmony, discord, and dishonoring found in the world. The world has an allure, but it is shallow. There is something within us that longs for something true and deep.

Homer's Odyssey describes the tempting sound of the Sirens, luring sailors into their rocky shallow waters that would sink their ships. In his book, *One Thing*, Sam Storms spoke of Ulysses who had his sailors wear earplugs so as not to be distracted by the Sirens, while he commanded them to strap him to the mast with his own ears unplugged so he could hear their song. That is the picture the world often has of the church—tying ourselves up yet really wanting what the world has to offer—with no idea that there is something far more enthralling that they need to hear. Storms then talks about another person in the story: "Jason, like Ulysses, was himself a character of ancient mythology.... Again, like Ulysses, he faced the temptations posed by the sonorous tones of the Sirens. But his solution was of a different sort. Jason brought with him on the treacherous journey a man named Orpheus...a musician of incomparable talent.... When it came time, Jason declined to plug the ears of his crew. Neither did he strap himself to the mast.... He chose a different strategy. He ordered Orpheus to play his most beautiful and alluring songs. The Sirens didn't stand a chance! Notwithstanding their collective allure, Jason and his men paid no heed to the Sirens. They were not in the least inclined to succumb. Why? ... Because they were captivated by a transcendent sound. The music of Orpheus was of an altogether different order.... Jason and his men said 'No' to the sounds of the Sirens because they had heard something far more sublime. They had tasted something far sweeter.

They had encountered something far more noble" (pp. 126-127, used by permission). We have in our hands a far sweeter song than that found in our world, one that rings true and deep. The world has a tendency to dance to something—maybe it is because music is deep within each of us. Let's give them something amazing: the sound of heaven!

God's voice is indeed powerful. It created all things. And, at the most fundamental level, those things, including our physical beings, may be reminiscent of the vibrations of His voice which spoke them into being. How fitting it is, then, that we would offer these "vibrations"—that is, all that is within us—back to Him as true worship unto the Lord. It's music that He loves to hear.

7
Partnering with His Voice

In the last chapter, we saw the power of God's voice: it can shake the earth; it can change the course of human lives; it brought the world into existence. It may seem incomprehensible that we can partner with this aspect of God, but this is something that Scripture tells us is absolutely true.

Praying Like Jesus

We may have learned to pray for healing something like this: "Dear Lord, if it be Thy will, please heal my brother down here. He's a good man, compared to a lot of people. Amen." When we look at the healing prayers of Jesus, they are quite different. Most don't even seem like prayers!

"Receive your sight." *(Luke 18:42)*

"Ephphatha!" *(which means "Be opened!")* *(Mark 7:34)*

"Get up, take your mat and go home." *(Luke 5:24)*

"Lazarus, come out!" *(John 11:43)*

These are not petitions; rather, they are commands. They are akin to God speaking at the creation of the universe, *"Let there be light!"* (Genesis 1:3). First comes the word, then God's action. One might ask, didn't Jesus speak this way because He was God? Should we be praying like this? As I discussed in Chapter 3, Jesus did not take advantage of His divinity when He ministered, but ministered in a way that could be a model for us. Just as He used such commands, He told His disciples to do the same:

> *"Truly I tell you, if anyone says to this mountain, 'Go, throw yourself into the sea,' and does not doubt in their heart but believes that what they say will happen, it will be done for them."* (Mark 11:23)

And later we see His disciples praying this way, too:

> *Then Peter said, "Silver or gold I do not have, but what I do have I give you. In the name of Jesus Christ of Nazareth, walk." (Acts 3:6)*

> *Turning toward the dead woman, he said, "Tabitha, get up." She opened her eyes, and seeing Peter she sat up. (Acts 9:40)*

When Jesus prayed like this, people recognized that Jesus was operating in authority. This authority He has given to us as well. For example:

> *"I will give you the keys of the kingdom of heaven; whatever you bind on earth will be bound in heaven, and whatever you loose on earth will be loosed in heaven." (Matthew 16:19; see also Isaiah 22:21-22, where keys again represent authority.)*

To see these sorts of commands in the Old Testament, consider this vision in the Book of Ezekiel:

> *The hand of the Lord was on me, and he brought me out by the Spirit of the LORD and set me in the middle of a valley; it was full of bones. He led me back and forth among them, and I saw a great many bones on the floor of the valley, bones that were very dry. He asked me, "Son of man, can these bones live?"*
>
> *I said, "Sovereign LORD, you alone know."*
>
> *Then he said to me, "Prophesy to these bones and say to them, 'Dry bones, hear the word of the LORD! This is what the Sovereign LORD says to these bones: I will make breath enter you, and you will come to life. I will attach tendons to you and make flesh come upon you and cover you with skin; I will put breath in you, and you will come to life. Then you will know that I am the LORD.'"*
>
> *So I prophesied as I was commanded. And as I was prophesying, there was a noise, a rattling sound, and the bones came together, bone to bone. I looked, and tendons and flesh appeared on them and skin covered them, but there was no breath in them.*
>
> *Then he said to me, "Prophesy to the breath; prophesy, son of man, and say to it, 'This is what the Sovereign LORD says: Come, breath, from the four winds and breathe into these slain, that they may live.'" So I prophesied as he commanded me, and breath entered them; they came to life and stood up on their feet—a vast army. (Ezekiel 37:1-10)*

As Ezekiel spoke these things, the Lord moved on behalf of his words. God knew what He wanted to do, but He wanted someone to speak it first. This is one of the ways we partner with

God in ministry. There are times when our part is to speak, and even as the echo of the words is still in the air, He moves. This is not to say we never ask God for things, but prayers of command are one of the ways God has given us to minister, such as when we are praying for healing. It is the same idea as the prophetic-like commands in the Lord's Prayer that we spoke of in Chapter 3: *"Your kingdom come. Your will be done on earth as it is in heaven"* (Matthew 6:10). Sometimes God calls us to express in words what He wants to do, then He acts—He has chosen it to work this way.

Prayers of command, like the prayers of Jesus, are directed at whatever needs to be changed. We are not commanding God; rather, we are expressing His will. What is His will? Look at the ministry of Jesus: He proclaimed the kingdom, healed the sick, released the captives, and told His disciples to do the same (Matthew 10:7-8). Unlike the concept of prayer being directed toward God, this is directed from Him, or on behalf of Him, such as speaking to parts of the body to be healed or pain to go. This brings up an interesting question: are these commands prophetic expressions of what He is saying to us at the time, or are they our words based on a general knowledge of what He wants to be done? The answer is *both*. Like a police chief and his officers, He has given us authority to bring the kingdom. We don't need to constantly ask the chief what to do when we see a criminal robbing a store—we just intervene. However, unlike this analogy of a policeman and his chief, we are filled with God's presence and are constantly in tune with His voice and heart, accessible to His telling us the best way to approach each situation. So, we have both a general sense of the ways of the King burning within us, yet also hearts and ears receptive to His heart and voice.

We are like Elijah, Ezekiel, and the prophets of old who were told to speak words that were precursors to the move of the Lord. The results were demonstrations of God's reality and power, toppling the enemy's gates and giving the people a hope in God, whose arm was not too short to save them. Our God is that God—the same yesterday, today and forever. We can do the same (James 5:17-18) if we realize who we are, seek to be in relationship with Him, and, as His Spirit moves with power, speak what He is saying and do what He is doing.

Other Types of Prayer

There are other types of prayer we might employ as well. We might simply converse with God. Or we might use *petition*, which is asking Him for things. Daniel, who asked for God's help, was told by an angel some days later: *"Your words were heard, and I have come in response to them"* (Daniel 10:12). Asking for God's presence is a form of petition. And here is one of my favorites: "Help!" Sometimes, during ministry, you just don't know what is going on and need some help!

Intercession is about our role as a mediator. A mediator is someone who comes between two parties and explains to one what the other is saying and vice versa, bringing them together. In prayer ministry, we are bringing a person to God and God to a person. The Hebrew word for intercession is *paga*, which also means "to meet." In prayer ministry we come before a person and God, essentially saying, "Let the meeting begin!"

Prophesying

Another way we partner with God's voice is through prophetic ministry: hearing what He is saying and speaking those words to others. This is normative Christianity! Both in the Old Testament and New, there are over 2100 verses showing God speaking to people. Christianity is about a relationship between God and man, a relationship initiated by a desire so strong that the Father gave His Son in order to draw us near to Him. As in any relationship, communication is important. Can you imagine a relationship without it? Or a relationship where one partner did all the talking and the other only listened? Neither partner would like that.

God can speak to us in numerous ways. The Bible itself is our main means of hearing from God. It is His clear and undisputed voice and our sole source of doctrine. However, we often need specific direction for specific situations, especially when we want to do His will in ministry settings. The Bible was not written to be a list of specific instructions for every circumstance we might ever encounter. (That's probably not even possible and, even if it were, in the natural realm we often don't know what all the circumstances are.) The Bible does give us general instructions, yet it also portrays God as one who will speak to us about specific details in our life and show us the way. Looking at His relationship with Moses and David, for example, we can see that He loves His people near to Him, praying, asking, talking, and listening to His voice. He wants us to draw close.

Some say that we are now in the New Testament age and no longer in the age of the prophets; therefore, prophecy is a thing of the past. But in 1 Corinthians 12-14, Paul talks about gifts for this age, many of which involve hearing from God (that is, they are prophetic in nature). I would argue that prophecy is to be more prevalent in this age than ever before. Our age is the answer to the cry of Moses, *"I wish that all the Lord's people were prophets!"* (Numbers 11:29). The time in which we now live is a fulfillment of Joel 2:28-29 as quoted in Acts:

> **"In the last days, God says, I will pour out my Spirit on all people. Your sons and daughters will prophesy, your young men will see visions, your old men will dream dreams. Even on my servants, both men and women, I will pour out my Spirit in those days, and they will prophesy."** *(Acts 2:17-18)*

In 1 Corinthians 14:1, Paul exhorts us to eagerly desire to prophesy, which he says again in 1 Corinthians 14:39, showing how heartfelt his yearning is that we desire this gift.

Paul lays out purposes of the prophetic ministry in several places throughout the New Testament. In 1 Corinthians 14:3, he says prophecy is for *"strengthening, encouraging and comfort."* Thus, a prophetic word can speak to our present situation, giving us strength; to our past, giving us comfort; or to our future, encouraging us to go forth. In 1 Corinthians 14:24-25, Paul writes that prophesying can cause unbelievers to come to God, causing them to *"fall down and worship God, exclaiming 'God is really among you!'"* In other words, prophecy has a powerful role to play in evangelism.

To grow in hearing God's voice, first of all, ask for it. Realize that His sheep hear His voice (John 10:27 NKJV). Next, be attentive to the ways He may speak. (Someone once looked in Scripture at all the different ways God has spoken to people. The list became so long that he finally concluded that God speaks to people in every conceivable way!) God may "pop" words, pictures, or a verse into your mind. Or you may suddenly just "know" what God is saying. Sometimes He speaks through physical sensations, such as when Jesus perceived a flow of power going out from Him as a woman touched the hem of His garment for healing (Luke 8:46). God may let you feel His heart. He may speak through visions and dreams. If God gives you part of what He is saying, ask Him about it… He may give you more. Or share that piece…maybe it will make sense to the hearer. Get feedback in order to grow in accuracy. Always make sure that what you share reflects the heart of Jesus and is not contrary to anything in His Word. Finally, find others who wish to grow in this gift and get together and try it out. There are also many excellent books on the subject to help you move forward and avoid pitfalls.

A word you get may not seem significant to you at the time, but it may to the hearer, or maybe later its meaning will become clear. My son-in-law Ken recently gave someone a word that his refrigerator was going to break down, but that it would be a sign that the Lord was going to make things in his life like new. A month later that person's refrigerator did break down. I've never heard of someone being so happy that his appliance broke! But the person was happiest because he knew God was about to renew some things in his life.

Putting These Together for Ministry

I have found that for effective ministry, such as praying for the sick or injured, three things are the most useful. Before I get to those, let me say that overarching it all is *love*. Whatever we do must be a demonstration that God is here and that He cares. Revealing His loving heart can do more than heal bodies; it can transform lives.

The first element, as described in Chapter 5, is ministering with **His presence**. It is interesting that in Genesis 1, both God's presence and word came together, with the explosive result being that the universe was born. In ministry, His presence is the first thing I ask for, and I am continuously aware of Him as ministry progresses. If I feel the Spirit intensify, especially after a word is spoken, I won't change direction for a while. That is indicating to me what He is doing, and my desire is to follow Him. It is *His* ministry, and it is an honor to take part in the beautiful things He does.

The second element is realizing our authority and praying like Jesus did, often using **prayers of command**. Whatever it is we are praying for, I know it is God's will to bring people's bodies and minds into the ways they were designed to operate, so I speak to those things to conform, whether it is for pain to be gone, swelling to reside, or cells to function properly. As prayer progresses, I often ask the person to check out how they are feeling (sometimes on a scale of 0 to 10), perhaps asking them to do something they could not do before. This helps us not to quit too early (it's ok to pray again!) and also encourages us and them when we see that things are changing. It also shows the person that we believe results to be real and testable.

The third element is using **prophetic words and insights**. These can be given for the person's encouragement and well-being. (As prayer ministry begins, I usually ask God what makes this person special to Him. This prepares my heart and theirs for what is about to happen and sets an atmosphere of His love.) Also, in the case of ministering physical healing, seeing or hearing prophetically can help us know what to pray for and where to direct our prayers of command. I found that often, the more specific a command is, the more effective it tends to be. So, when praying for neck pain, for example, the Lord may show someone a picture of the person's neck, perhaps highlighting swollen tendons, so that is what we speak to. As prayer continues, I prophetically discern if there are any underlying causes to pray for. (Sometimes there is something underlying and sometimes not...a person may just be sick because they are sick.) If what we are praying for is physical, that calls for one type of prayer. If it is emotional or spiritual, that calls for another type, such as discerning a lie they have come to believe (for example, feeling worthless because of what an authority figure told them at an early age). Here we need to counter the lie with God's truth, which He often has us speak prophetically. If there is more than one thing to pray for, I ask God what to do first— He knows the best place to start.

Ministry at West Aurora High

A story that encapsulates this type of prayer happened at the high school near where we used to live. Christina Tammen, an amazing teacher there, holds a Bible group that meets after school once a week. The group invited me to come and do a series of equipping classes. In the final session, I talked on authority and healing. Christina had invited some students with injuries to come. One student was one of the school's top wrestlers who had severely injured his knee. He didn't know the Lord (yet). He came in a little late just as we were looking for someone for whom to pray. So, the students zeroed in on this wrestler who was standing there on crutches wearing a knee brace.

We had a girl who had known the Lord for just several weeks put her hand on his knee. Then we asked the Holy Spirit to come. As soon as we did that, the girl jerked her hand back saying, "What was that? It was like a buzz! Oh, that must have been his cell phone going off." But we had the wrestler check his cell phone and it had not gone off. So, she put her hand back and we kept going.

Everyone was commanding the knee to be healed and the pain to go, and every so often we would have him check his pain level. The pain dropped significantly, so we prayed again. He had started out in immense pain and soon it was gone. He couldn't believe it. Then we started having him check his leg motion. He had virtually no motion when starting. Now he could move it 20 degrees with no pain! Only his knee brace was keeping him from bending it further. The students asked him to take it off. Erring on the side of caution, I said, "Don't do anything against your doctor's orders," but he went ahead and took it off anyway. Now he could bend it 90 degrees with no pain. He was amazed. He started doing deep knee bends. Part of me wanted to stop him, but the other part was thinking, "This is so cool!"

Then we had him show us his knee, which was swollen with his kneecap off to the side by about an inch. The students prayed again with everyone watching. I was standing behind him and could not see, but the students gasped as the swelling went down and his kneecap moved back into place. He got up and walked around, squatting down with no pain! Charlie, one of the students whom I would best describe as a walking revival, said to him, "What God did to your leg He wants to do with your life. Do you want to give your life to Him?"

He said, "Sure!"

A week later the wrestler visited his doctor. The doctor walked in holding two x-rays, one from when he was injured and one from that day. He said, "I can't explain this!" It was as if he had a new knee.

I am so taken with how much the Lord is upon all of the students in this group. Even a year later, almost every day they would lead someone to the Lord or pray for someone who was healed. Apparently, the Lord likes to attend West Aurora High!

It is a privilege to partner with the Lord in this way, and He constantly shows us how best to do it. We know that He cares deeply for people, and when we see this occur in ministry situations, we ourselves are often so touched by His goodness that we are changed, desiring to devote our lives to His cause, that we may see this happen again and again.

We partner with Him in many ways: with His presence, His heart, and His voice. There is no one like our God, whose words are filled with love, power, and creativity. He who spoke words to create the world also speaks them to us. And He loves to use *our* voice in speaking His words to others. That is amazing!

Part IV

Energy

8
God, Energy and Motion

If you think that God's timelessness means His realm is motionless and involves nothing new, you have wrong ideas about Him. God being timeless simply means He is outside and unaffected by time as we know it—He is eternal—He always was and always will be. His unchangeability (He *"does not change like shifting shadows"* – James 1:17) is about His character—His goodness—not that His world involves no change. He is creative, and that always involves change. In eternity, we will forever watch His creativity and goodness unfold and be equally as astonished in the first year we are there as in the millionth year. Of course, change, expressed in the terms of energy and motion, is an integral part of this world as well.

The Science of Motion and Energy

Besides time, space, and matter, another important ingredient of the universe is the motion and energy it contains. Sitting outdoors on a warm, starry night, things may seem still and peaceful, but nothing is actually as static as it seems. The oxygen molecules in the air are moving at an average speed of 1,070 miles per hour, the earth is traveling in its orbit around the sun at 67,000 miles per hour, and the sun is traveling in its trajectory around the galactic center at a whopping 515,000 miles per hour. And in your body, the cells are in motion, rapidly processing fuel and replacing parts of the cell—every year 98% of the atoms in your body will have been replaced. I truly am not the man I used to be!

Energy can be thought of as the ability to change things or set them in motion. The energy associated with motion is called *kinetic* energy. A compressed spring is not necessarily moving but has the ability to set something into motion, so it has a type of energy which is called *potential* energy. Potential energy can be mechanical (as in springs or water towers), chemical (as in gasoline or batteries), or nuclear (as in reactors or stars). Heat is another form of energy due to the motion of molecules. And energy can also be converted into mass and vice versa according to Einstein's $E=mc^2$ (energy = mass times the speed of light squared).

Energy is also found in waves, such as light. In creation, the first thing God spoke was *"Let there be light,"* and there was light (Genesis 1:3). The universe began with an unimaginably powerful burst of energy, containing all the energy and mass in the universe today. The energy was eventually converted into other forms of energy: fueling stars, giving rise to nuclear and chemical power, and putting into motion all that is in the universe.

[Note: It is interesting that in John 1, Jesus is described as both the Word and light, both of which provide illumination, dispel darkness, and were integral in creation. Light, in all its colors and forms, also displays beauty, something which both creation and Jesus' words do in remarkable ways. And in heaven, God Himself will provide light: *"There will be no more night. They will not need the light of a lamp or the light of the sun, for the Lord God will give them light"* (Revelation 22:5). That will indeed be beautiful.]

Motion in Scripture

Scripture actually has a lot to say about motion, sometimes in unexpected ways. A while ago, at a church near the Wisconsin

River pastored by a good friend of mine, I had a strange thought: What do you think God likes better: lakes or rivers? I had no idea, but I thought it would be fairly easy to find out. Just look up all the verses that mention lakes or rivers. I found that God had rather strong opinions on which He likes better!

In pursuing this thought, I first discarded references to actual lakes and rivers. I don't think God has an opinion about those. The verses in which I was interested were those where lakes and rivers were used as symbols or allegories. Used symbolically, what is the difference between lakes and rivers? Both involve water, but the major difference is that in rivers, the water is moving. It shows change and is capable of carrying a person from one place to another. So, a river would symbolize something that is flowing, moving, and changing. A lake would symbolize something that is standing still.

I began with references to rivers. In two of those references, Isaiah 43:2 and Luke 6:48 (where the Greek word for *torrent* can also be translated *river*), a river depicts the flow of everyday life. It can change; it can move us; but it can also sweep over a person in a way not always to his or her liking. Often, we try to make our lives into lakes, trying to keep everything still and unchanging, only to discover it really is a river, with its swells that can sweep over us and with its bends where people can become stuck.

Most of the references to rivers, however, depict the river of God. It can symbolize the Holy Spirit, as in John 7:

> **"Whoever believes in me, as Scripture has said, rivers of living water will flow from within them." By this he meant the Spirit, whom those who believed in him were later to receive. (John 7:38-39)**

Rivers can also symbolize the flow of God's delights or attributes, such as peace, justice, and righteousness (see Psalm

36:8, Isaiah 48:18, and Amos 5:24). The river of God brings a fresh unfolding of His goodness, changing us and taking us somewhere.

The only references to lakes, however, were in Revelation 19:20, 20:10, 20:14-15, and 21:8, all of which refer to the lake of fire: constant, never-ending turmoil. Definitely not a positive connotation! So I began to see that, symbolically anyway, God prefers rivers over lakes.

One of the most interesting references to a river is in Ezekiel 47:1-12, the river flowing from the temple of God. It starts ankle-deep and becomes deep enough to swim in. Life grows in it and along its shore. These are the verses we discussed in Chapter 3, which describe heaven (the kingdom of God) being poured out on the earth. What is fascinating, however, is this verse:

> *"But the swamps and marshes will not become fresh; they will be left for salt." (Ezekiel 47:11)*

Why is this water being left out? It's because its water is not moving! Therefore, it does not come in contact with and become refreshed by the moving river of God. Again, God has a preference for moving water!

The last reference to rivers is also interesting. It is found in the last chapter of the Bible, where heaven is being portrayed. And what is there in heaven? A river!

> *Then the angel showed me the river of the water of life, as clear as crystal, flowing from the throne of God and of the Lamb.... On each side of the river stood the tree of life.... And the leaves of the tree are for the healing of the nations. (Revelation 22:1-2)*

So, what is God's preference for rivers trying to say? These verses tell us that His world—and who He is—is something which is in motion; it is continuously fascinating, as we watch the unfurling of His creative beauty. His very presence is like a moving river. Even heaven will not be stagnant, but a continual unfolding of God's goodness. That is what we can expect!

As we have seen, there are two rivers talked about in Scripture: the river of everyday life and the river of God. In the river of everyday life, people can get stuck in its bends, where that river has taken unexpected turns. If we can get into the river of God, however, it can help us be freed from those bends where we are stuck in life. Life is a river, and we may just as well get used to it. But rather than just being pushed around by that river, God invites us to jump into His river and be taken on the adventure of our lives, always changing, constantly taking us to the spiritual places where He would have us go next.

Our Call to Be in Motion

Just as God is a Being in motion, so we are called to be the same. Simply gathering information about God yet remaining stagnant in our lives is not what He has in mind for us—God desires that we be doers of the Word, not just hearers (James 1:22). It would be sad to miss out on the adventures that lie ahead of us if we were never to take action. This is Daniel's revelation of what is available to us:

> **But the people that do know their God shall be strong, and do exploits. (Daniel 11:32, KJV)**

The word "do exploits" (literally "do") is also translated as "take action." It is true that Jesus commended Martha's sister Mary for sitting at His feet. The disciples did that, too, and it is essential that we often do likewise—that must be a pursuit like none other. (We must first concentrate on "being" God's beloved and loving Him...and only from there flow to "doing.") However, Jesus also invited them to go out with Him as He proclaimed and demonstrated the kingdom of God. In the Book of Acts, His followers were filled with the Spirit and began saying what Jesus said and doing what He did. Even the name of that book—*Acts*—speaks that the disciples were in action. It is interesting that the book of Acts ends suddenly, almost as if to say that we are still writing it and doing the acts!

In making disciples, we must concentrate on more than just teaching. If the church were a sports team, teaching would make us knowledgeable spectators, but Christianity was never intended to be a spectator sport. Teaching is essential, but we must also take to the field. Besides teaching, we need equipping, training, trying things out, and deployment.

The Church was designed to be a place of amazing diversity in backgrounds, cultures, gifts, and callings. This can only happen if we value unity. But for this to happen, it is also essential for the Church to be in motion, affecting our world. As an illustration of why this is so, certain people might be gifted at playing basketball, but without a game in motion, they cannot use their gifts. So, too, in the Church to which many gifts have been given, without it in motion we not only lack a place for *our* gift, but we also cannot see how our gift interacts with *other* gifts and how much we need one another. One time, while at a pastor's conference, I saw a picture in my mind of a sideways "V". It reminded me of a flock of geese flying in formation. The "V" was the front line of the church as it moved across the world and encountered the lost. Superimposed on the "V" were all the various gifts: apostles at the tip, evangelists, prophets, and worship people on the lines, and pastors, teachers, and healers just behind to take care of those who were coming into the kingdom. All the gifts fit amazingly well into this picture. Each was critically needed. As soon as the "V" stopped moving, however, this formation disappeared, and no one knew what to do with many of the people or their gifts. With the Church in motion, every gift has its place, and we all honor one another as we move toward a common goal, seeing how much we need every person and gift. There is power when we work together. Although one can put a thousand to flight, two can put ten thousand to flight. However, this can only be seen when we come into motion; without it no one is being used.

Power in Science and Scripture

Early scientists, such as Sir Isaac Newton, transformed the somewhat vague concepts of force, energy, power, etc. into precise mathematical formulas and definitions. Power is the rate at which energy is used to do work—that is, to change things or set them into motion. It is interesting how close this is to the Scriptural use of the word *power* (*dunamis* in Greek). For example:

> *"But you will receive power when the Holy Spirit comes on you; and you will be my witnesses in Jerusalem, and in all Judea and Samaria, and to the ends of the earth." (Acts 1:8)*

Notice that power is connected to a purpose, to change things and set things into motion—in this case, to be Jesus' witnesses. The experience to which Jesus was referring here (which we call the baptism of the Holy Spirit) has this purpose of effecting change: first in us, then spreading outwards to others. Therefore, if we are to take full advantage of this encounter, it must be on our hearts not just to say that we have had this experience, but also to be propelled by it to effect change and set things into motion. How this will unfold may not become obvious until sometime later in our lives, but we at least need the understanding that what we have received will enable us for action.

This verse also connects power to the presence of the Holy Spirit. The Holy Spirit is not optional—we need Him! He was given to fulfill what Jesus would have us do. To think we can do His work with our own strength is prideful. Worse yet, we don't want to be found having a *"form of godliness but denying its power"* (2 Timothy 3:5), as Paul warned would happen in the last days. The Holy Spirit is available to all who would ask (Luke

11:13). To make sure we are partnering with the Holy Spirit properly and doing His work well—revealing God's presence, power, heart, words, and character—look at the ministry of Jesus or turn to the book of Acts. These are not just of historical interest...they are models for our lives. We can't miss the opportunity to effect change and set things into motion!

Power in the Church: Ingredients for Revival

Just as individuals have the privilege and mandate to be endued with God's Spirit and power, so does the Church. If we, the Church, are not at the place we should be in this, we should ask for it. Over the centuries, God has visited His Church with revival, displaying what it should be like. To some extent, revival happens because it is God's chosen (*kairos*) moment to visit us. But another element in its coming is our realizing what we have been given and walking in it. I feel one of the greatest moves of God is at our doorstep. To steward this well, we must be prepared. Here are some ingredients for walking in revival:

- ***Prayer, Desire, and Repentance***: The greatest revivals have been preceded by the greatest times of prayer. Among other things, prayer is expressing our desire for God and for Him to move. We must see the state of the world and know that He is able to change it. In the past He has done just that—and we need it to happen again. Part of this is turning from (repenting of) our sins and shortcomings, personal and corporate, and embracing God, His forgiveness, and His help. We need to surrender all that God wants to replace in us, as He fills us with His presence and directives for what lies ahead.

- ***Encountering God***: It seems that today the Western Church is too satisfied with gathering knowledge (e.g., listening to good sermons) but not actually encountering God and then being set into motion. As I said in Chapter 1, we are too complacent in being second-generation rather than first-generation prophets. I once heard an illustration accredited to Søren Kierkegaard which involved two doors in heaven: one labeled "Lectures about God," which had many waiting to go in, and another simply labeled "God," which had only a few in line. According to the parable of the prodigal son, I think the father would be a little disappointed if, after having redeemed his son, his son were to choose "lectures about the father" over the father himself. Moses was not satisfied until he encountered God, and then walked close to Him the rest of his life. We need that same heart. Revivals always have included encounters with God—they are transformational. *We* need these, too—many times in our lives (Acts 2:1-41, Acts 4:23-31).

- *Knowing our Identity*: One of the things that keeps people from moving with the presence and power of God is not knowing their identities in Him. Like the lion son in the movie *The Lion King*, they don't go into action because they don't know who they are. God has given us amazing identities. Before Gideon became a warrior-leader, the Angel of the Lord spoke these words to him: *"The LORD is with you, you mighty man of valor!"* (Judges 6:12 NKJV). Although that may not have been true of Gideon just yet, when God establishes our identity, the way we then see ourselves is what we become.

- *Coming against the Enemy's Lies*: The enemy will try to confuse, distract, and stop us through lies that are either spoken or thought. The lies might involve what others think of us or come from our own thoughts and insecurities, making us question our own identities and callings. We need to know this is a strategy of the enemy and come against it. That is why the prophetic ministry is so important. One of the ways to combat lies, both personally and corporately, is to speak to ourselves and to one another the truths of God. Steve and Wendy Backlund have written about some powerful ways to do just that (such as in their book, *Declarations*). We need to encourage people often, because the world, the enemy, and sometimes even the Church have a way of draining people and taking their eyes off of who they are and what they are called to do.

- **Unity**. Whether it comes to our marriages, friendships, or churches, the enemy uses the strategy "divide and conquer." We mustn't let him do that. We need unity. If there are cracks in our unity, when revival comes, the enemy will try to end it by taking hold of those cracks and ripping us apart. We need to develop a culture of honoring one another. In his remarkable book, *Culture of Honor*, Danny Silk applies honor to many aspects of our walk: it strengthens us individually, establishes our unity, and better equips us to affect our world (which is currently saturated with the dishonoring of one another). He describes how, even when it comes to disciplining people, we must protect their identities rather than giving them the identity of being a failure. Such honor has been shown to bear remarkable fruit; it is the way the Bible says to treat one another. Applying this notion of honor to the way we support our community could bring revival to a whole new level, as the world experiences firsthand what it is like when heaven touches earth.

- **Tenacity**. Perhaps the most important attitude to have in moving forward is *tenacity*. Such a heart attitude is evidenced in Matthew 11:12: *"...the violent take [the kingdom] by force"* (KJV). Or, as it is expressed in the Amplified Bible: *"...a share in the heavenly kingdom is sought with most ardent zeal and intense exertion."* It takes a forceful grasp to lay hold of the advancing kingdom, and it takes tenacity to keep pushing ahead. Tenacity is important for launching into any ministry. We mustn't be afraid of failure; we must take risks (a characteristic of first-generation prophets). John Wimber said that he prayed for the sick for nine months without seeing anything happen. Then, once it started happening, it came like a waterfall and he became one of the most effective teachers in instructing others to do the same. However, he needed tenacity to begin and then to persevere. The college I attended offered skiing lessons as part of its curriculum. I took these classes every winter, and during my last two years there, I had a former Olympic coach, Fred Lonsdorf, as an instructor. I noticed how often he fell as he tried new things. One of his favorite sayings was, "When you're falling, you're learning." That was a lesson in tenacity! It takes tenacity to start out, but it also takes tenacity to keep moving. One time, as I was doing ministry training on the East Coast, I was driving along feeling a heightened sense of God's presence. As I fell asleep in my hotel room that night, I still felt Him. However, in the morning I felt the gloom of the enemy. So, I said, "Lord, where are you? What happened?" I heard Him say, "You've been pushing forward the front lines of the kingdom. Don't you think the enemy is going to push back?" That was true. Then He continued, "But when the enemy pushes back, you must push back even harder." So, I asked, "What should I do?" At that, I felt His presence fill me. I don't know how to describe it other than to say it felt like a lion inside of me. So, if the enemy pushes back, which he is bound to do, push back even harder! That is power in the form of *tenacity*.

- *Walking in God's Presence and Displaying His Heart*: One of the things I love about ministering is experiencing God's nearness and presence. Such will be the case in revival. It is, and should be, what we treasure most; do not let personal ambition ever take first place. Like the person who sold everything in order to purchase the treasure in the field, once you experience this presence of God, nothing else will do. The other thing I love is the way He will display His heart through our heart. When people encounter the heart of Jesus, even when reflected in the hearts of believers, lives are changed. Nothing moves me more than when, as we pray for others, they see Him. I'm sure we have all thought, "What must it have been like to see Jesus minister?" Here, in a small way, we get to know what that is like as people respond to His presence, power, and heart. There is nothing like seeing His heart and presence change the lives of others.

- ***Getting Ready for People Coming into the Kingdom***: When revival hits, the number of people coming into the kingdom will swell. We must be ready for this. We need people who are ready to pastor them, teach them, and bring healing to their wounds. We also need to equip these newcomers so that they can take their own places in the ministries to which they are called.

God has given us the opportunity to be in motion. And the key to doing that is to remain in Him. The Holy Spirit is indeed like a river: flowing, changing, and giving life. We have the opportunity of a lifetime to flow with it—to flow with *Him*. Become filled with His power and action. Be prepared for exploits beyond your wildest dreams. Such is life in His ever changing—but constantly good—kingdom.

Part V

The Realm Outside the Natural

9
Science vs. Christianity

For about 150 years there has been a seeming conflict between science and Christianity. It might seem rather esoteric and not worthy of our attention, but this battle has affected the Church at large and us individually, since we are part of its culture. It has, to a degree much too large, put the Church in a defensive mode and robbed us of some valuable possessions. It's time we instead move forward with a full knowledge that God is all He says He is.

Nineteenth Century Scientific Objections to Christianity

By the 1800s a scientific revolution had come into full swing. Scientific terms had precise mathematical definitions and physical laws had precise mathematical formulations. The scientific method (where one postulated a theory, developed tests for it, and then verified those tests in the real world) became the universal guideline for adding to the scientific database. Indeed, it was revolutionary. Superstitions, such as draining sick people's blood (bloodletting) to remove their "bad blood" (a misguided practice responsible for numerous deaths, including that of George Washington), fell by the wayside as proven medical techniques vastly improved healthcare. Knowledge of the cosmos and its physical laws lead to many advancements, eventually even putting a man on the moon. Science had earned a great deal of respect in all fields of study.

As of the late 1800s, scientists felt confident that most scientific laws had been discovered with just a few loose ends to tie up. Little did they know that the scientific advancements of the 1900s were soon to undermine this confidence. However, before that, some used this mindset to take aim at whatever they deemed as non-scientific. In the late 1800s, the implications of the scientific revolution were used by some to deem Christianity as non-scientific and therefore useless. Here are some of their assertions:

- ***Reality is solely material.*** Reality consists only of matter and energy which obey the set laws of science. Therefore, everything is subject to the scientific method, which alone produces a reliable set of knowledge. Things that are not testable, such as superstitions, have no part in this. The supernatural (including God), they said, also falls into this category.

- ***The universe had no beginning.*** At that time, the universe was believed to be in a steady state, having no beginning. Therefore, there was no place to talk about anything (or anyone) that caused a beginning.

- ***Scientific laws explain all mysteries of the universe.*** Looking at the universe, the laws of science—not God—made it the way it is. You are looked down upon if you disagree.

- ***Darwinian evolution explains how man came about.*** Darwinian evolution (random changes in biological systems, with "survival of the fittest" keeping the changes that are for the good) explains how all life, including man, came about through natural processes. And the environment of early Earth accounts for how primitive life began.

- ***Humans are purely material.*** The laws of nature account for everything pertaining to who we are. There is nothing spiritual about us.

- ***The supernatural is not scientific.*** Like superstition, science will show that the supernatural is not real.

Conclusion: There is no need for God.

Many of these points have been refuted by science itself over the past 120 years. (Other points are just based upon bad logic.) Even though the science behind them is outdated, some of the arguments are still being made today. In the past 120 years, knowledge has come to light that really does show the fingerprints of God on the universe as the One whose unfathomable intelligence designed it all. I will discuss this later in this chapter. But first let me discuss the reaction of the Church to this, much of which still affects us today.

The Reaction of the Church

Some parts of the Church (what we refer to as liberal theologians) embraced these points, not wanting to be considered "backwards." In academic settings, science enjoyed a great deal of esteem and respect, and people in other fields of study sought the same respect by applying the same logic to their areas. So, these parts of the Church, rather than embracing all of Scripture as being true, such as the verses that speak of God's supernatural activity, started seeing some of Scripture as mythology or allegory, or assumed it was written to promote the agenda of various social classes, since class struggle was popular in sociology at the time.

Other parts of the Church drew back from all this and circled their wagons, defining and defending the "fundamentals" of their faith (hence the term *Fundamentalist* movement). Their academicians spent their energy building tight systems of logic around their beliefs, and the churches enjoyed the resulting comprehensive theological systems, feeling safe within their borders. (There is nothing wrong with comprehensive theological systems as long as we don't make them our sole focus or, inadvertently, trust in our own interpretation of the Word more than in the Word itself.)

The subject that seemed to be most prone to the debates of the day was the supernatural activities of God. This seemed to be the hardest tenet to hang onto while maintaining one's respect, especially in academic communities, where many withdrew from it. Some in theology held onto the supernatural events in the Bible, while others did not (some liberal theologians dismissing any supernatural claims, even the resurrection). Others took a "middle" ground, trying to explain the miracles in the Bible with natural means (which was a bit of a stretch in most cases).

As far as present-day supernatural activity goes, not surprisingly, the liberal theologians dismissed it. However, even the conservative proponents distanced themselves from it, since they were much more comfortable with their predictable logical systems, with modern-day supernatural activity seeming too unpredictable and uncontrollable. [Note: For more on this and other subjects in this book, click on the *Extended Notes* link at *SecondRefPress.com*.]

Interestingly, the Pentecostal revival arose at this time, which was immersed in the supernatural but did not have the respect of many. Yet it went on to spur (both directly and indirectly) an enormous growth of the Church, with sizable contributions in Africa (whose Christian population progressed from 9 million to 380 million between 1900 and 2000). Since then, more "waves" of Spirit-empowered movements which have embraced the supernatural have arisen, affecting the world significantly. Now it seems that more groups than ever are embracing God's supernatural acts, as these acts are becoming increasingly evident.

Back around 1900, both science and the Church stood their grounds with their arms crossed. (To be more accurate, I should say *some* in science, since there have always been significant scientists who have embraced the faith, and *some* in the Church, since not all reacted in the ways I described.) Some felt the best resolution was for science to claim its ground (the physical universe), and Christianity to claim its ground (God and His interaction with people), but never the two shall meet. I remember that even I, when I was a college professor, had somewhat of this "two worlds" approach, although I did share stories of how God would break His own laws of nature to show His love, which was His greatest priority. Looking back, I can see how the "two worlds" approach does not give enough attention to the ways God's fingerprints are all over the physical universe. (I did talk about the "Anthropic Principle," which is discussed below.) I felt that, perhaps, God had hidden His reality so that we would seek Him out of love, not through our discovery of information. There is a bit of truth to this, but it is not completely true. As with everything else, the Bible had the proper point of view all along.

The Heavens Declare the Glory of God

Although in some ways God hides Himself so that we seek Him out, in other ways His fingerprints are more plainly seen in creation than we may think. We cannot simply dismiss His realm as being entirely outside of the physical universe, with no interaction within. God says this:

> *The heavens declare the glory of God; the skies proclaim the work of his hands. (Psalm 19:1)*

> *What may be known about God is plain to them, because God has made it plain to them. For since the creation of the world God's invisible qualities—his eternal power and divine nature—have been clearly seen, being understood from what has been made, so that people are without excuse. (Romans 1:19-20)*

Scripture therefore tells us that there *is* evidence of His interaction with the universe. Personally, what really drew my attention to this was Lee Strobel's book *The Case for a Creator*. As in all his books, he looks at the issue from all sides, utilizes impeccable research, then presents his case. I would highly recommend reading this book to gain more understanding of some of the points made in this chapter. It made me realize how much more the heavens and the earth proclaim the work of His hands than I had previously appreciated. There is no doubt that creation declares the glory of the One who created it.

Problems with the Nineteenth Century Scientific Objections to Christianity

In light of all this and what we now know, let us look more closely at the nineteenth century scientific objections to Christianity listed above and explore how they are either outdated or logically flawed.

- **Problems with "Reality is solely material"**: By definition, the material universe *is* solely material. But that does not mean that reality is confined to the material universe. No one can say that.

Even if we were unable to see something, that does not mean it does not exist. There are things in the physical universe that we cannot see and, for some time, did not know existed, but now we know they do. For example, we cannot see "dark matter" in the universe, but only recently realized it must exist to explain the structure of galaxies.

Scripture, however, says that we *are* able to see evidence of God in this world: the heavens declare it! And indeed, this is true. Just looking at the universe, which we know had a beginning, leads us to realize that something outside of it had to create it. Looking more closely, the fingerprints of a Creator, which reveal an overwhelmingly well-thought-out design, are seen throughout creation. And beyond this, His supernatural activity can often be clearly documented and its after-effects examined, just as well as any other event that occurs in the world.

- ***Problems with "The universe had no beginning":*** This is an example of something that was believed in the 1800s but was later refuted by science in the 1900s. Around 1964, it was discovered that the universe was created in an unimaginable burst of energy, which was verified by the detection of the remnant of its light that is now background radiation. Also, light from stars exhibits a Doppler shift (similar to what we hear from a train whistle, which is at a higher frequency when a train approaches us and a lower frequency when it moves away from us). If a star were moving away from us, the frequency of its light would become lower (shifted toward the red part of the spectrum). It turns out that the farther stars are from us, the faster they are moving away from us—signs that the universe is expanding. So, a major dispute with the Scriptural assertion that the universe had a beginning suddenly vanished. The universe *did* have a beginning...which poses the question: What or Who caused it to begin?

- ***Problems with "Scientific laws explain all mysteries of the universe":*** Many of the laws of physics involve "fundamental constants" such as the strengths of the four fundamental forces (which are electromagnetism, gravity, the strong force, and the weak force), the mass of the particles (such as electrons, protons, and neutrons), and the initial conditions of the universe (such as the total number of particles in it and its expansion rate). No one knows why each of these have the numerical values they do, but around 1970, someone asked and researched what the universe would be like if their values were different. The results were astonishing. If they were even *slightly* different, not only could there be no life as we know it, but the universe also could not support life of any kind. Consequently, it became evident that not only do the scientific laws fail to explain all the mysteries of the universe (such as what started it), but the scientific laws present a mystery themselves. It seems the universe is "tuned" so that life—and we—can exist! (Thus, the name "Anthropic Principle" was given to this.)

Going into some detail, the study found that if the relative strengths of the four fundamental forces were not just right, you could have no life-sustaining stars and also no carbon in the world. (No carbon means no us!) If the ratios of the particle masses were not just right (within a fraction of a percent), there would be no atoms and very little hydrogen in the universe, so no planets and no us. And if the force of the explosion when the universe was created was not just right (within 0.000000000001 percent = one part in a hundred trillion), the universe would have been too short-lived or expanded too quickly for planets to have formed. Some have estimated that there may be over thirty fundamental constants. If you can imagine a control panel with thirty dials, each having to be set to an *amazing* precision, then you can see how much the universe is "tuned." How did this happen? The best explanation is that there is a Tuner! The Nobel Prize-winning scientist Arno Penzias said this: "Astronomy leads us to a unique event, a universe which was created out of nothing, one with the very delicate balance needed to provide exactly the conditions required to permit life, and one which has an underlying (one might say 'supernatural') plan" (from his *Thinking about the Universe* address of 1983, quoted in *The Case for a Creator,* p. 161).

- Problems with "Darwinian evolution explains how man came about": Living organisms, and even cells, have been found to be far more complex than what was thought in the late 1800s when Darwin postulated his evolutionary theory. With our most advanced technology, the world's most knowledgeable engineers have tried for years to build nanomachines with tiny motors capable of simple functionality. Cells are like nanomachines, but much, much smaller, with way more functionality than any of the ones we know how to build. And they can reproduce! Each part of a cell is astounding, and when seeing how these all function together within the cell, it is absolutely mind-boggling. Their complexity and precision make their creation via evolution astronomically unlikely, if not impossible. Often, cells contain interacting subsystems that defy Darwinian evolution, because each subsystem can do nothing useful without working in conjunction with other fully functional subsystems. Therefore, they could not have evolved via survival of the fittest—they were not fit for anything until they and the other subsystems were highly developed. There is simply no evolutionary explanation for how all these parts became highly developed.

Living creatures such as ourselves contain trillions of cells (we contain 37 trillion), the interworking of such being *so* amazing and complex that the likelihood that they came from anything random is about zero. Each part of the body is a masterpiece, with a marvelous design. Not only that, but the entire human body can reproduce, starting with a single cell, through the instructions in that cell's DNA. The complexity involved is almost incomprehensible! George Sim Johnston wrote, "Human DNA contains more organized information than the Encyclopedia Britannica. If the full text of the encyclopedia were to arrive in computer code from outer space, most people would regard this as proof of the existence of extraterrestrial intelligence. But when seen in nature, it is explained as the workings of random forces" (from his *Did Darwin Get It Right?* Wall Street Journal article, October 15, 1999, quoted in *The Case for a Creator,* p. 231).

As for the origin of life, the theory that Darwinian evolution can account for it is now in doubt by some of the leading minds on the subject. Even Franklin Harold, a biochemist unfriendly to the idea that there was an intelligent Designer, acknowledges: "We must concede there are presently no detailed Darwinian accounts of the evolution of any biochemical system, only a variety of wishful speculations" (from his *The Way of the Cell*, Oxford University Press: New York, 2001, p. 205, quoted in *The Case for a Creator,* p. 204).

Francis Crick, of Watson and Crick (winners of the Nobel Prize for the discovery of the structure of DNA), having a similar disposition as Franklin Harold, admits the origin of life is not as automatic as some had supposed: "An honest man, armed with all the knowledge available to us now, could only state that in some sense, the origin of life appears at the moment to be almost a miracle, so many are the conditions which would have had to have been satisfied to get it going" (from his *Life Itself*, New York: Simon & Schuster, 1981, p. 88, quoted in *The Case for a Creator,* p. 44).

It is odd that, in school or most anywhere else, we never hear about the critical questions evolution leaves unanswered, giving us the impression that it is an iron-clad, problem-free explanation for life. What we now know about the cell and the human body points much more to the idea that these were exquisitely designed. Personally, I want to pay homage to the One who created something so magnificent.

- Problems with "Humans are purely material": It is difficult to put a person under the microscope to see whether or not something non-material exists, because microscopes can only detect physical things. Nevertheless, there is some evidence that our consciousness surpasses the boundaries of the brain. (See *The Case for a Creator,* pp. 261 ff.) Perhaps significant are some of the near-death out-of-body experiences that have been documented, such as a surgical patient who saw things on the hospital roof that she could not have known about without being there, which may indicate that there is something non-physical about us. (For experiences like these and all others, make sure Scripture is your ultimate authority.)

Most compelling to me, however, is the way we each experience our own consciousness, which would serve no purpose in a purely physical system. I think in heaven we will realize how ridiculous the notion is that a human is only physical; if each person were only a physical "machine," why couldn't it walk around and do all it does without us?

- ***Problems with "The supernatural is not scientific"***: In a sense, this is true; science only deals with things that are physical and repeatable. The supernatural, by definition, is outside the natural realm. And supernatural events are also one-time occurrences, not things that can be repeated in a laboratory under a scientist's control. However, that does not mean they are not real or cannot be verified. In another book by Lee Strobel, *The Case for Miracles*, he cites numerous examples of miracles that have been well documented.

Studies have shown the effect of prayer is quite real. A researcher, following missionary Heidi Baker in Mozambique, found *dramatic* effects as she prayed for people's hearing and eyesight, sometimes resulting in complete or nearly-complete healing of deafness and blindness (*The Case for Miracles*, pp. 133-135). Much of the time, when I pray for healing, I see definitive changes, but my focus is more on the person than on having them obtain proof of what happened. (Once in a while I hear reports that their doctors verified the changes, not always being able to explain what they saw!) So, from my perspective, the well documented cases of the supernatural are only a fraction of what actually occurs.

Back to Our Future

If there was once a war between science and Christianity, I say that it is over! Some seem to have an interest, in promoting their own agendas, to say that it is not. They can live in their own worlds if they like, but to the rest of us, we need to move on.

To those in the Church with their arms crossed and wagons in a circle, I say: Come out of your defensive positions. Look forward to the journey ahead. Embrace all that was stolen from you, including the supernatural activity of God. The supernatural is natural for God. If God wants to use it to show He is real and He cares, who are we to say that we know better? If God used the supernatural in the book of Acts, why would He stop? Jesus used it extensively, explaining that He did what He saw the Father doing (John 5:19), so it is clearly important to God.

Even as I have been writing this chapter, a friend shared his story in our church of how he came to the Lord. Part of his beautiful story began with a tragic event. As he was walking across his college campus one evening, three men attacked him, one striking him repeatedly with a large metal pipe. In the hospital, doctors examined his head and discovered severe trauma and broken bones. They informed him that he probably would not live through the night. As he lay in his bed, he realized he didn't know God, who He was, or even how to address Him, but he asked God to show him who He is and to come to him and help. Just before he fell asleep, he saw a vision of Jesus at the foot of his bed. The next morning, the doctors examined him and found him to be completely healed. They told him that his recovery unmistakably was a miracle. My friend was so thankful to have been healed—but was even more overwhelmed that he had been visited by the One he now knows is God, to Whom he gave his life.

We must not let the world or anyone else put blinders on us as to what God and His kingdom are like. We must open our eyes to God and let *Him* show us what He is really like, and let the limitations of what He can do fall to the floor.

Recent science is showing people that there may be more to reality than what they see in the everyday world. And people are reacting, wondering: Is there more to life than what they have assumed? Now is the time to show them that there is. God *is* real, and He cares about them more than they could think or imagine.

10
Seeing the Supernatural

Living in a culture that has dismissed the supernatural has affected our ability to see it. One of the reasons may be that a lack of belief in something (due to being told what we can expect or not expect, either by our culture or the church) can actually affect what we see and hear. Supernatural activity can be going on in front of us, but unless we are attuned to it, we can dismiss it before it registers in our minds.

The effects of our culture's anti-supernatural bias upon us can be reversed, however. But how can we do that personally?

Paradigms and Our Views of the World

The connection between believing and seeing can be discussed in terms of *paradigms*. The way sociologists often use the word, a *paradigm* can be thought of as the way we model the world in our minds—the way we believe it works. For example, we may believe the supernatural activity of God can happen, or we may believe it cannot. Both are paradigms. This "believing" is not just what we *say* we believe, however. It is what we *expect* will happen. So, the closest concept to the way that I'm using *paradigm* is *expectant faith*: how we expect the world to work.

It has been found that our paradigm affects the way we view the world, influencing what we "see" and don't see. I put "see" in quotes because our eyes actually see everything around us, but the complexity of images that come at us are preprocessed by our minds so that we can concentrate only on what we think is important. For instance, when we drive a car, we may not notice different shades of gray in the pavement ahead of us because we believe (through experience) that they are not important. That information is filtered out at a low level in our seeing process so that other information, such as a child playing near the street, can attract our mind's fuller attention. When someone from the South moves to the colder climates, however, the first time they hit a patch of ice on the road they may be in for a *paradigm shift*: they had not believed that the subtle shades of gray in the road's appearance were important and did not really "see" the icy patches in the road ahead. When they realize how important those variations on the roadway can be, they suddenly start seeing those different colored patches. Their paradigm shifts, affecting the way they view the world.

I found that the same thing happened when I began shopping for a particular brand of car. Before I became interested in buying a Mazda 3, I could have sworn that I had never seen very many of them on the road. Once I became interested in them, however, it was amazing how many I began to see! Although I previously believed that Mazdas existed, I did not feel that they were very important. When that "belief" (paradigm) shifted, my view of the world (and the cars in it) changed!

Years ago, the teens in our church befriended a young man named Danny. Danny spent most of his time on the streets. A severe head injury as an infant had affected him mentally. One of his endearing qualities was the way he would quote clichés—usually a little mixed up. For instance, "I'll believe it when I see it," would always come out as "I'll see it when I believe it." We loved that, because we realized that with the things of God, Danny's words were much closer to the truth. In the language of paradigms, Danny's saying would come out this way: "My view of the world will change (I'll see it) when my paradigm begins to shift (when I believe it)."

This is true of the supernatural acts of God. Without the right paradigm, we can fail to see and act upon the supernatural promptings of God. God can give us a prophetic revelation, but if we are not attuned to the fact that He might speak like that today, we can dismiss His thoughts before they even enter our minds. Or, if they do enter our minds, we might just attribute them to insight and not give them another thought. Even miracles can be missed by those without the necessary paradigms and eyes to see them.

Sometimes merely hearing someone talk about the extraordinary ways God operates is enough to begin shifting our paradigms. This shows us something interesting: Not only do our paradigms affect what we see, but what we see can affect our paradigms (our expectant faith). So, once we start seeing something new (such as someone talking about miracles), our paradigms can shift, causing us to see even more, which can cause our paradigms to shift even more, and so on. It's a snowball effect! Shifting paradigms can cause our lives to be shaken for a while, but we end up with a new and exciting view of the world. Those things we begin to see are, and always have been, real, but now our eyes are opened, and we are more fully aware of the diverse ways God acts.

The Shifting Paradigms in the Gospel of Mark

In my first book, *The Presence, Power and Heart of God*, I showed how shifting paradigms and views of the world can be seen in the Gospel of Mark. (Many thanks to my exceptional seminary professor Louis Brighton for pointing this out.) This provides a clue as to how we might shift our own paradigms.

Even though the word *paradigm* is not found in Scripture, the Gospel of Mark is filled with dramatic examples of changing paradigms. The book of Mark is a short, action-oriented account of the ministry of Jesus. Most of the verbs in the original Greek are in the present tense and get the reader caught up in the action and experience of being with Jesus. Because of the immediacy of the text, it is easy to put ourselves in the shoes of the people as they reacted to all that was said and done. Their reactions to Jesus' words and works can be viewed as a progression which Mark often describes through variations of the word *amazed*. While *amazed* may be connected with the people's emotional state of mind, Mark uses it to point us to the radical underlying change in the way the people thought about God and their world—radical shifts in their paradigms! For the reader, Mark's intent (and God's) is for our expectant faith to grow (our paradigms to shift) and our eyes to be opened. At one point, Jesus, frustrated that the disciples still had their old mindsets even after seeing many miracles, said, *"Do you have eyes but fail to see, and ears but fail to hear?"* (Mark 8:18). He is chiding them for not seeing as they should, all because their faith (paradigms) needed to change. His intent is that we would see and therefore believe—and believe and therefore see!

If you look up *amazed* in the *Englishman's Greek Concordance* (its index will point you to *amazed* and all of its synonyms), you will find fourteen occurrences in the Gospel of Mark. Placing them in the order they occur, the forms of the word *amazed* (as shown by the words of their English translations) increase in intensity.

In Mark 1:22 they were amazed at Jesus' words. In Mark 1:27 and 2:12 they were amazed at His works. In Mark 5:42 they were *"completely astonished"* (NIV) or *"astonished with a great astonishment"* (KJV) at His raising a girl from the dead. In Mark 6:2 they were amazed at His wisdom, and in 6:51 were *"completely amazed"* (NIV) or *"sore amazed"* (KJV) at His walking on water. In Mark 7:37 they were *"overwhelmed with amazement"* (NIV) or *"beyond measure astonished"* (KJV) at a miraculous healing.

Mark 9:15 contains the most intensive form of *amazed* in biblical Greek (found only in the book of Mark). Just after the

Transfiguration, Jesus approached a crowd gathered around His disciples who had failed to cast out a mute spirit from a man's son. As the crowd saw Jesus, they were *"overwhelmed with wonder"* (NIV), although they had not yet seen Him do anything or heard Him say a word. Why such an intensive form of amazed when nothing had happened? Some have speculated that He was glowing from the Transfiguration, but Scripture does not say this. It only says they saw Him. I believe their paradigms had been so shifted with each act and word of Jesus that they had previously experienced, that now Jesus did not have to do or say anything to cause their expectancy to surge—He only needed to be seen. This is where Mark is trying to take us. When, in their desperation, they suddenly saw Jesus walking toward them, they now had eyes to see that He was all they needed. "Jesus is here! Anything can happen!" So it is with us as we progress in the shifting of our paradigms and the growth of our faith, thereby changing our view of the world. We learn by experience who Jesus is and what awesome things can happen when He comes.

The action-packed part of Mark ends with Mark 16:8. It is followed by a twelve-verse epilogue written in a separate style. The change in style sets the epilogue apart from the rest of the book. Therefore, imagine a long pause as the original hearers are left hanging with the emotion of what they heard as Mark 16:1-8 ends: the stone is rolled away, an angel says, *"He is risen! He is not here."* and then, *"So they went out quickly and fled from the tomb, for they trembled and were* **amazed***. And they said nothing to anyone, for they were afraid"* (Mark 16:8, NKJV). This form of amazed (translated *bewildered* in the NIV) is so intense that it has an element of fear and bewilderment. Some scholars wonder how Mark could end on a note of fear. I believe this was not ordinary fear, but the apex—the culmination of the amazement of what the people had been experiencing— the ultimate in paradigm shifts as they saw the empty tomb. As the disciples saw the tomb's emptiness, their jaws dropped as if to say, "If He is not here, where is He?!" If the reader's attitude in Mark 9:15 was, "Jesus is here! Anything can happen!", now it had become, "Now He could be anywhere and come at any time!" Mark, in fact, leaves us with faith for the era in which we now live. By God's presence, He now *can* be anywhere and come at any time. We are left astonished, our paradigms shifted, ready and expecting the amazing works of the kingdom to happen at any time.

Eyes to See: Tips for Seeing More of the Supernatural

To acquire eyes to see, our paradigms need to shift. One way for that to happen is to listen to stories of supernatural occurrences from others. In *The Case for Miracles*, Lee Strobel presents a survey he commissioned, which found that thirty-eight percent of the adults in the United States have experienced a miracle (p. 30). Unfortunately, our culture and even some of our churches have not been conducive to the sharing of our experiences. People have been too leery to talk about them, which has led to a lost opportunity for others around them to grow. So, just ask your friends if the miraculous has ever happened to them. They might be as eager to share their experiences as you are to hear them, and as they do, your own eyes can be opened.

There are also numerous books, videos, and movies to help in this regard. Darren Wilson's movies, such as *Finger of God, Father of Lights*, and *Holy Ghost*, walk through his own story of seeing his paradigm shift as he sees—and captures on film—God do some amazing things.

Another way to develop eyes to see is to find opportunities allowing supernatural acts of God to occur. There is nothing like experiencing these things for yourself. For this to happen, we often have to experience something new. That involves risk. Faith, by its nature, involves risk—to walk the walk of faith, we must step out and do things we would not be able to do without

God. In the story of the servant who buried his master's money to keep it safe (Matthew 25:14-30), the master, when he returned, was furious that the servant had not taken a risk. The moral of this story is that when it comes to God, it is riskier not to take a risk than it is to take one! The heroes of faith mentioned in Hebrews 11 all had this in common: They were risk-takers. Even society's modern-day heroes tend to be people who have taken risks. But we are not supposed to just admire people like this; we are supposed to *be* a people who take risks ourselves.

Moving out in a spiritual gift or praying for someone for the first time can seem like a huge risk. In teaching people how to minister, one of John Wimber's favorite sayings was, "Faith is spelled R-I-S-K." So, in ministry, try things that may be new for you, whether it be sharing a prophetic word with a friend or praying for someone to be healed. For me, the things we do in ministry still sometimes seem like a risk. But it is always a risk worth taking.

Taking a risk can seem like jumping off a diving board—it's scary on the climb up; it's scary when we jump off. But these are the places where the supernatural acts of God seem to come. And after we've jumped, the feeling of being in the water is great. Through such risk-taking, we are bound to see the supernatural...that's just the way it works. And once we have seen it, our eyes will be opened to seeing it even more as our paradigms, and thus our views of the world, shift.

Revival at FM 92

To illustrate how paradigms can shift, I share a portion of a story that happened at a Christian radio station in January 1995. Earlier in the day the station had interviewed Randy Clark, a man used by God to trigger an exceptional move of God. Later, the Holy Spirit began touching the staff members. The station manager, Jon Hamilton, told listeners what was happening, after which some of them began showing up at the station. Jon writes:

> The crowd continued to grow, and lines began to form. The power of God continued to fall on those coming. It was almost like being in a dream. I would look up and see our staff members, eyes red, faces puffy, and hands trembling, but with a fire in their eyes and the power of God upon them. I couldn't believe it was the same people I knew and worked with. In a matter of hours, something we never even dreamed of (much less aspired to) was happening....
>
> At some point I looked up and saw a local Baptist pastor walk in the door. I must confess that my first thought was "Oh boy...I'm in trouble!" While I knew this brother to be a genuine man of God, nevertheless I was concerned about how a fundamental, no-nonsense Baptist might take all that's going on. (Besides, I didn't have an explanation to offer!) I walked up to greet him. He just silently surveyed the room, and with a tone of voice just above a whisper said, "This is God. For years I've prayed for revival. This is God."
>
> Within minutes more local pastors began to arrive. Lutheran, Independent, Assembly of God. The word of what was happening spread like wildfire. As the pastors arrived, they were cautious at first, but within just minutes, they would often begin to flow in the same ministry. The crowd was growing, and pastors began to lay hands on the seekers, where once again the power of God would manifest and the seeker would often collapse to the ground.
>
> It did not seem to matter who did the praying. This was a nameless, faceless, spontaneous move of God. There were no stars, no leaders, and frankly, there was

no organization. (It's hard to plan for something you have no idea might happen!) ...

Amazingly, unchurched, unsaved people were showing up. I got a fresh glimpse of the power of radio as person after person told us, "I'm not really a part of any church...." A few were skeptical at first, and later found themselves kneeling in profound belief.

Sometimes people would rise up, only to frantically announce to us that they had been healed of some physical problem. One woman's arthritic hands found relief. Neck pains, jaw problems, stomach disorders and more were all reported to us as healed.

We have received at least a dozen verified, credible, reliable comments from people who told us that when they switched on the radio, they were suddenly, unexpectedly overwhelmed by the presence of God (even when they didn't hear us SAY anything). Several told us that the manifest presence of God was so strong in their cars that they were unable to drive and were forced to pull off the road....

It's hard to imagine the impact this has had on our staff. It seems like God has almost given me a new staff, composed entirely of men and women with tremendous zeal for God.

What is occurring in our local churches is even more amazing. My phone is ringing with the calls of excited pastors. At least a dozen area churches from completely different ends of the theological spectrum are already experiencing this powerful move in their church. The leaders of many, many other local fellowships have been visiting these churches to "check it out," and they, too, are being touched to "take it back" with them. It's a lot like a tidal wave has hit this area of Florida.

If you are skeptical, I understand and forgive you. (I might have thrown a letter like this one away just days ago.) I share this only to try and offer a faithful rendition of what has really happened.

I only ask that you remain open to whatever God wants to accomplish through you. Christian history is full of accounts of those times when God elected to "visit" His people. When He has, entire nations have sometimes been affected. I believe you'll agree; our nation is ripe for such a revival. For such a time as this, let us look to God with expectancy. (From Jon Hamilton's letter to his constituency, January 1995. Used by permission.)

Jon's closing words could not have been better said: "For such a time as this, let us look to God with expectancy." May we have eyes to see all that God can do and look to Him, expecting Him to do it—in our world and in our day.

11
What is Most Important to God

God designed the universe carefully and brilliantly, with finely tuned physical laws that determine the behavior of the physical substances of the universe. He could violate these laws at any time. But does He?

It depends on what is most important to Him.

God's Highest Motivation

Scripture states what is most important to God. It is love. (Some may answer this question slightly differently—relationships, God's heart for the lost, His glory, His goodness—but the conclusion I draw in this chapter will be the same.) It was love that prompted Him to create us in the first place. He delicately tuned the entire universe in order for us to live. He created a world of extravagant beauty, excited to share it with us whom He so magnificently made. His longing was to fellowship with us—for Him to love us and for us to love Him. It was love that characterized the vibrant relationships He had with so many of the champions of the Bible—from Adam to Moses to David to Jesus to Peter and John—all of which show the kind of relationship He wants to have with us all. And it was love that prompted Him to send Jesus, who would endure a most torturous death so that we could have a relationship with Him. It is love that, even now, extends an invitation for us to live in His very real and exceedingly beautiful kingdom. God is love (1 John 4:8).

The life of Jesus was the most exact representation of God's character ever to be seen on the earth. Jesus said He came because *"God so loved the world"* (John 3:16). And that love motivated everything Jesus did, including miracles of every sort. Those miracles broke the laws of the universe, because doing so would show people God's reality and love for them, and that was more important to God than maintaining the physical laws.

Roots

At the end of every school year, I would tell a story to my physics classes at Valparaiso University—a story which took place in the very room where those classes were held. It involved Jack (not his real name), whom a friend and I had met earlier. Jack had a tragic past. His father left him and his mother shortly after he was born; then a few years later, his mother died. He went to live with an uncle who never accepted him and abused him with beatings. All his life he struggled to find roots in this world but could find none. Doing some research, he found out who his natural father was, but in visiting him, this man would have nothing to do with Jack, telling him that he had barely even known his mother.

I remember toward the end of one of my physics classes, I saw Jack wander into the back of the room. When class was over, I asked him if he would like to join me for lunch. The two of us walked across the street to where my friend Tom worked, and the three of us then walked to the McDonald's next door. As the three of us sat at a table, talking about the Lord, I saw a woman come toward us from the other side of the restaurant. I'll never forget how she took off her sunglasses and slid them on top of her head. Then she looked directly at Jack and said, apologetically, "I'm sorry to bother you. But I was sitting over there, and I felt the Lord say to tell you, 'If you are to come to

God, you should come like a child coming to his father.'" She apologized again and left.

I asked my friend Tom who that was. He said, "I have no idea....I thought you might know." I didn't know either. That left Jack undone. God was offering to be the root Jack never had. But breaking the laws of the universe in order to tell him this—that is what impacted Jack the most. God will break any law of nature to show His love—that is His highest priority.

I still don't know if that woman was a person or an angel. If she was an angel, it must be that angels prefer white minivans, because that is what the woman drove away in.

Since then, I have had many, many experiences in which God violated physical laws in order to heal people, encourage them, or show them He is real. All of this is out of His immense well of love for them.

How Often Can We Expect This?

In talking about this, the question arises: how often can we expect this sort of thing to happen? I don't really know the answer, but I suspect it is more often than most of us think.

Whatever supernatural activities of God we are seeing now, I think God wants to do more. He calls us to ask for and expect more, just as Jesus did with His disciples (John 14:12-14). Also, I think we are on the verge of a move of God which will bring a great many people into His kingdom, and His supernatural activity will be a large part of this. In fact, this has already begun.

Besides the obvious supernatural events that get our attention, however, there are others that are subtle yet still miraculous. God's creation of the universe and of life (both actually not so subtle!) really are supernatural. And I believe that sometimes He sustains these in ways that are supernatural, although we do not always recognize Him doing so. He sustains us as well. We may not even be aware, until we get to heaven, of all His supernatural intervention that protected us from harm. Also, there are times when He speaks to us so subtly that we often take it as intuition, until it becomes very obvious that it was Him. My son-in-law Keith, a talented designer, has twice now woken up in the middle of the night with an idea for the design of a logo for some organization. He would then create the logo and email it to the organization's leader. Both times, those people said they had just prayed for a logo design when suddenly, Keith's email appeared in their in-boxes!

What if we pray for the sick or injured but God does not supernaturally intervene? Sometimes we can trace it to a particular reason, but other times this is not the case—we simply don't know. In such cases we have to chalk it up to mystery and not become too paralyzed to continue on. (That, however, doesn't mean we shouldn't keep pressing into God for better strategies.) Robby Dawkins, a good friend of mine, has seen thousands of people healed. Yet after repeatedly praying for his mother to be healed, she died. Even while visiting her at the hospital, he prayed for a person with a similar condition in the room next door who was dramatically healed. That is hard for us to understand, although God understands completely. Our part is to continue to do what He said we should be doing (Luke 9:2) and leave the mysteries to Him.

We are living in a time when heaven is breaking in as we bring the kingdom, but it is not yet here in its fullness, as it will be at the Last Day—even nature is groaning for that time to come (Romans 8:22). God has inserted us into the drama of living in this universe and being subject to its laws, where events, by nature, are sometimes wonderful, sometimes difficult, and sometimes sorrowful. However, that is the same place where He is calling us to be shining lights, to show the world that He is here and He is good. There are times, like during the ministry of Jesus, where He asks us to call on the very laws of the universe to be bent in order that people may see His light. I live expecting this to happen at any time…in increasing measure.

God often sets the bar high in what we can expect Him to do. Some lower that bar just to agree with their experiences. It is more honest to keep the bar where Jesus set it and keep going after it, even though we may encounter circumstances that don't seem to meet our expectations along the way. My desire is to keep aiming for the seemingly impossible when God says it *is* possible. Already, we've seen things that some would say could never happen. As we step out in these things, we will see them again and again.

Picturing His Love

If God's highest priority is love, then our highest priority should be to move into a life of increasingly loving Him. I've often wondered how to do this better.

I have found that when I think of any relationship—whether it be with my wife, family, or friends—I tend to have a mental picture of what the relationship is like. For example, when thinking about my wife, I often picture a particular photograph of the two of us at our wedding reception, a side view of us looking into each other's eyes; it is something forever pressed onto my mind. A while ago, I felt I needed to do this with my relationship with God. Although we do not have any physical images like we do with our spouses or friends, it is still something we can do, since Scripture itself paints pictures of Him. It is interesting that Scripture does not just tell us *about* God, but it also conveys many stories of people's experiences that involve God. That makes it easy to put ourselves in the shoes of the people in those stories, feeling what they must have felt. I even like to take the verses of Jesus conversing with people and try to verbalize what Jesus said with the inflections He may have used, just so I can let my mind match with what He may have been thinking. In this, we can create a more accurate picture of Him in our minds.

In forming such a picture of our relationship with God, although there is no one verse that gives us a complete picture, we can draw from a lot of verses across Scripture, each one giving us a brush stroke of a more complete portrait. Looking at verses about Jesus, sometimes it's what He says or does, and other times it's the reaction of people, such as the woman washing His feet with her tears, or crowds spending all day just to listen to Him speak. They show how much He must have touched their hearts.

Of course, our own personal experiences with God, or watching Him minister to others, also paint a picture of God in our minds. Unfortunately, hurtful experiences with authority figures (or other people we have encountered) can sometimes paint negative pictures about God until we find, through Scripture or the ministry of other believers, what God is really like, and we remove any false pictures of God we have been carrying around. It is also good to have friends who have a close relationship with Jesus and who accurately reflect Him to us and to the world. These, too, can help us obtain a better picture of Him, as we see Him reflected in those who love Him.

Here are three pictures of God that have risen to the forefront for me. I expect that everyone will picture Him in their own unique ways, but hopefully this will inspire you in painting pictures of your own.

Picture 1: Jesus the King. Jesus has unparalleled majesty, but also unparalleled accessibility. It is hard to find an example of this combination in the world, but Scripture clearly shows both. In teaching us how to pray, Jesus portrayed God the Father with this same combination of attributes: *"Our Father in heaven..."* (Matthew 6:9). The first two words, *"Our Father,"* show His closeness to us; the next two words, *"in heaven,"* show His awesomeness—God fills the heavens, yet He is as close to us as a father. Romans 8:15 uses the term *"Abba,"* denoting a close, intimate relationship between a father and his child. It is a term of endearment, deeply personal, best translated as "Papa" or "Daddy." So, picturing Jesus as a majestic king, yet one who is also our friend, is completely Scriptural. It's important to keep both attributes in mind; one enhances how amazing the other is.

My first picture of Jesus is that of a king...the One who walked the earth, gracing the world with His presence and reflecting the nature of His kingdom. That kingdom was described by His words and demonstrated by His works. It brought freedom and life and light. Everyone could see that it was good—that was unmistakable. The truth, however, is that the *kingdom* is so good because the *King* is so good. Having seen its goodness, then, confronted everyone with a question that needed to be answered: Do you want to be in this kingdom? Do you want Jesus to be your king? That question is more important than any other in this life. Answering "Yes" changes everything.

There have been many people in my life that reflected Jesus. One was a person named Jerry Jantzen, whom Mary and I met quite a few years ago. I considered him a walking revival. Now he is the pastor of a fruitful ministry in Japan. When I first met him, I could see genuine love and care in his eyes, as if to express to everyone he met, "You're amazing." Words about God's goodness came naturally bubbling out of him. He had a unique way of sharing insights on how to better our walk with God. Almost instantly he became one of my best friends. When I envision what Jesus was like, I often think of Jerry; that's what Jesus must have been like, but probably a hundred times more so, not to mention a majesty like none other that coursed through Jesus' being.

Now back to my picture. Imagine yourself in a large gathering, and you meet someone new who is like our friend Jerry, giving you the same reaction. Imagine that later, someone comes up to you and says, "Do you know who that person is you were talking to? That's the King!" Light bulbs go off in your head. "Oh, my goodness, no wonder the kingdom is so good! I felt so loved talking to him. I want in! Enough of the disappointing kingdom of this world. I want *Him* as my king!" That is my first picture of Jesus...*the good King.*

Picture 2: Jesus the Sacrifice: Some people may picture Jesus this way, but ultimately turn His kingdom down because they feel they aren't good enough—they feel they don't fit. What they don't realize is that no one felt good enough at first. Scripture is full of people that didn't seem to fit. Jesus said how hard it is for rich people to enter the kingdom, then a short time later He encountered Zacchaeus, a man rich by dishonest means, who suddenly was in (Luke 18-19). There were robbers like the thief on the cross, adulterers like the woman about to be stoned, and murderers like Paul who persecuted Christians. Making a mess out of things does not disqualify us...the kingdom and the King can change everything. If we would just tell Him we want Him to be our king, He would put His hands on our shoulders, wipe away all our sins and messes, and forgive us. What we may not realize for some time, however, is what that cost Him.

And this leads us to another picture I often have of Jesus: the very same king from the first picture, now on the cross. He suffered horrifically on our behalf. The same King I got to know and love—the one whose goodness was so hard to imagine—is now being put to death.

Hebrews 12:2 says that He endured the cross *"for the joy set before Him."* What was that joy? Astonishingly, *we* were that joy—as was the thought that we would always be safe with Him. So, the second picture is this: amid all His suffering, as we look into His face, He is thinking of us. We are the joy that is getting Him through.

Picture 3: Jesus our Groom: There is another picture I often have, especially when I attend weddings. It is set in an age yet to come, when we will be part of a wedding where Jesus will be the groom and we will be the bride, about to marry the desire of our hearts. One thing that always strikes me about weddings is the moment when the bride walks down the aisle, when every eye is upon her, seeing how beautiful she looks. For Jesus' wedding, *we* will be that bride. All the stunning angels of heaven will turn toward us in wonder as they see us. They will be taken aback by our beauty, although we will know we have been made beautiful by the magnificence of our king, wearing the robes of righteousness that He has given to each of us.

And then our attention turns to the Groom, who is intently watching us come toward Him. As we look at Him, we see the face of Jesus who is looking at us with such affection in His eyes, seeing us: the object of His long-time dream.

Ponder that. If you can picture what that face must look like, know this: that is the face that is looking at you now.

The Object of God's Affection

We are the object of God's affection. Having a close relationship to us is the dream He had all along. It is His deepest desire. Going back to the beginning of the Bible, it is interesting that in the first garden, man hid from God as God called out for him. But in the second garden, as the Bible and its remarkable story of our redemption comes to a close, we see the bride crying out to God, *"Come!"* (Revelation 22:17). Hearing us say that must bring tears to God's eyes, as He experiences His longtime dream coming true.

God's love for us can be unimaginable, yet it is real. For some of us, the place where we live—on this planet in this huge universe—can feel lonely. But the Creator of it all knows and loves us. As the mathematician and scientist Blaise Pascal once said, we were created with a God-shaped vacuum in our hearts that can only be satisfied by God Himself. If we would ask Him, He will fill that void. We can walk with Him in this life, be showered with His love, listen to Him explain all we see, and live as part of His remarkable kingdom, with mission and purpose.

This is the King who will bend heaven and earth, space and time, and every law of nature, in order that He might have us. Exploring the depth of this love will take us well into eternity to comprehend. But that is something worth exploring. If the physical universe is worthy of discovery, how much more is the realm of God? For the physical universe is only a tiny fraction of all that there really is. And our invitation to explore the rest is in our hands. That would be the noblest of endeavors.

Bibliography

Backlund, Steve. *Declarations: Unlocking Your Future.* Redding, CA: Igniting Hope Ministries, 2013.

Barrett, Eric and Fisher, David. *Scientists Who Believe.* Chicago, IL: Moody Press, 1984.

Fisk, Randy. *The Presence, Power and Heart of God: Partnering in His Ministry.* North Aurora, IL: Second Ref Press, 2006.

———. *The Amazing Word of God: Seminary-level Information Anyone Can Understand.* North Aurora, IL: Second Ref Press, 2010.

Johnson, Bill. *Face to Face With God: The Ultimate Quest to Experience His Presence.* Lake Mary, FL: Charisma House, 2007.

Ladd, George Eldon. *The Gospel of the Kingdom: Scriptural Studies in the Kingdom of God.* Grand Rapids: Eerdmans Publishing Company, 1959, 1988.

Lewis, C. S. *The Lion, the Witch and the Wardrobe: A Story for Children.* First published in London: Geoffrey Bles, 1950.

McManus, Erwin Raphael. *The Way of the Warrior: An Ancient Path to Inner Peace.* New York: WaterBrook, 2019.

Price, Charles. *The Real Faith.* Plainfield: Logos International, 1940, 1972.

Silk, Danny. *Culture of Honor: Sustaining a Supernatural Environment.* Shippensburg, PA: Destiny Image Publishers, 2009.

Storms, Sam. *One Thing: Developing a Passion for the Beauty of God.* Kansas City, MO: Enjoying God Ministries, 2004.

Strobel, Lee. *The Case for a Creator: A Journalist Investigates Scientific Evidence that Points toward God.* Grand Rapids: Zondervan, 2004.

———. *The Case for Miracles: A Journalist Investigates Evidence for the Supernatural.* Grand Rapids: Zondervan, 2018.

White, John. *When the Spirit Comes with Power: Signs and Wonders among God's People.* Downers Grove: Inter-Varsity Press, 1988.

Wigram, George V. *The Englishman's Greek Concordance of the New Testament.* Grand Rapids: Zondervan Publishing House, 1970.

Wilson, Darren. *Finger of God: The Movie.* Elgin, IL: Wanderlust Productions, 2007.

———. *Father of Lights: The Movie.* Elgin, IL: Wanderlust Productions, 2012.

———. *Holy Ghost: The Movie.* Elgin, IL: Wanderlust Productions, 2014.

About the Author

Randy Fisk received his Ph.D. in high energy physics from the State University of New York at Stony Brook based upon research at Fermilab in Batavia, Illinois. He also studied several years at Concordia Seminary in St. Louis, Missouri. He taught at Valparaiso University, then pastored with the Association of Vineyard Churches. For over 30 years, he has focused on helping other pastors equip their people to minister. Randy has spoken, ministered, and taught in various settings, always with an emphasis of having everyone experience the ministry, not just hear about it. His heart is to give away all he has and to see the Body of Christ mobilized in effective and empowered ministry.

Randy and his wife, Mary, live in Mapleton, Illinois. They have three daughters, three sons-in-law, and extremely wonderful grandchildren, all of whom are their delights: Holly and Ken (with Kinsey, Kalei, and Keith), Becky and Keith (with Judah, Rayah, Faith, and Viennah), and Mandy and Justice (with Corbin and Joab)!

Additional copies of this book or Randy's other books, *The Presence, Power and Heart of God: Partnering in His Ministry* and *The Amazing Word of God*, are available through online booksellers such as *Amazon.com*. To inquire about multiple-copy discounts (or however he can help), email the author at *RandyFisk333@gmail.com*. Extended notes are available by clicking on the *Extended Notes* link at *SecondRefPress.com*.

www.ingramcontent.com/pod-product-compliance
Lightning Source LLC
Chambersburg PA
CBHW070302010526
44108CB00039B/1643